Documento de Trabajo
Serie Política de la Competencia y Regulación
Número 65/ 2024

Artificial Intelligence and European Competition Law
(Inteligencia Artificial y Derecho Europeo de la Competencia)

Claudia del Olmo Van Woerkom

El Real Instituto Universitario de Estudios Europeos de la Universidad CEU San Pablo, Centro Europeo de Excelencia Jean Monnet, es un centro de investigación especializado en la integración europea y otros aspectos de las relaciones internacionales.

Los documentos de trabajo dan a conocer los proyectos de investigación originales realizados por los investigadores asociados del Instituto Universitario en los ámbitos histórico-cultural, jurídico-político y socioeconómico de la Unión Europea.

Las opiniones y juicios de los autores no son necesariamente compartidos por el Real Instituto Universitario de Estudios Europeos.

Los documentos de trabajo están también disponibles en: www.idee.ceu.es

Serie *Política de la Competencia y Regulación* de documentos de trabajo del Real Instituto Universitario de Estudios Europeos

Artificial Intelligence and European Competition Law
(Inteligencia Artificial y Derecho Europeo de la Competencia)

CEU *Ediciones*
Julián Romea 18, 28003 Madrid
Teléfono: 91 514 05 73
Correo electrónico: ceuediciones@ceu.es
www.ceuediciones.es

Real Instituto Universitario de Estudios Europeos
Avda. del Valle 21, 28003 Madrid
www.idee.ceu.es

ISBN: 978-84-19976-55-0
Depósito legal: M-25718-2024

Maquetación: Andrea Nieto Alonso (CEU *Ediciones*)

Summary

1. Introduction

Algorithm-based technologies such as Artificial Intelligence (AI) are increasingly pervading all areas of our lives. As a result, governments, policymakers, and competition authorities around the world have been grappling with the opportunities and threats that algorithms and AI pose. As the drawbacks of AI development and use come under closer examination, there's growing pressure on governments to implement not only policies encouraging positive innovation but also safeguards against AI risks. A well-designed regulatory system could not only foster trust in the technology but also promote its adoption, thus boosting countries' competitiveness. The advantages of establishing an effective regulatory framework for AI are particularly significant for regulatory authorities that move quickly to set standards.

This study delves into algorithmic cartels, pinpointing how they differ from conventional collusion. Its aim is to evaluate the emerging challenges stemming from the fusion of artificial intelligence and its interplay with European competition law. More particularly, the study explores tacit algorithmic collusion, identifying hurdles in their detection and proposing innovative solutions to bring them under existing legal frameworks. In pursuit of this goal, alternative approaches, such as reinterpreting certain legal concepts like "concerted practice", may yield a more comprehensive regulatory structure, thwarting attempts of innovative scenarios to evade legal scrutiny. Concurrently, algorithms present novel avenues to bolster competition and efficiency when utilized appropriately. Accordingly, an examination of these potentials is undertaken.

In pursuit of this goal, we will first assess the real impact of the different existing types of artificial intelligences onto European competition law and the available legal mechanisms to oversee them.

Secondly, a broad review of the different forms of collusion will in turn allows us to analyze the four most prevalent and concerning algorithmic scenarios for competition authorities, exploring how they might contravene existing competition legislation.

Additionally, we will focus on the existing legal mechanisms for detecting and preventing innovative algorithmic strategies that could harm consumer welfare and economic health, as well as new possibilities of determining accountability in such scenarios. Innovative interpretations of said established laws and legal frameworks may offer solutions to potential violations of competition law by artificial intelligence, often manifesting as tacit collusion. Nevertheless, it's crucial to acknowledge the potential advantages of algorithms in detecting and addressing potential cartels involving artificial intelligence, compared to human labor. While artificial intelligence poses significant risks to competition law and presents a formidable challenge for competition authorities, if utilized effectively, it can also serve as a solution to halt certain anticompetitive practices, particularly in oligopolistic and online market settings.

All of the above will be carried out with the support of an extensive bibliography, selected on the basis of relevance, timeliness, as well as the importance of its impact. Thus, the bibliography comprises primary sources such as jurisprudence, legislation, official documents from public institutions, technical reports, research surveys, etc. In addition, several secondary sources, including different legal scientific journals, manuals, books, newspapers, scholarly thesis, doctrinal works, relevant authors in the field, etc. have been consulted. However, it's worth noting that pinpointing ongoing research by competition experts to develop new policies and expand existing legal frameworks has proven challenging, primarily due to significant lacunae in insight concerning certain algorithms and their working schemes.

2. AI building blocks and competition law

2.1. Impact and relevance of Artificial Intelligence

Disruptive algorithm-based technologies such as Artificial Intelligence (AI) are progressively pervading all areas of our lives. Undeterred by the fact that no definition of "Artificial Intelligence" has been drawn up and universally admitted, the notion tends to be associated with the ability of technology to behave with the appearance of intelligence[1]. We regularly refer to AI which is already in widespread use, but it is equally pertinent to draw attention to AI that is currently still under development, and AI that is speculated to possibly exist in the coming future. In this context, we can identify three basic categories of AI: a first one composed of "weak" or "narrow" AI, in the sense that they can behave intelligently in domain-specific niches such as chess. An example of its application would be turning big data into usable information by detecting patterns and making predictions, as is the case with Amazon's suggested purchases or Apple's Siri.

Two further categories remain, although speculative and still non-existent: the so-called "strong AI", and "Superintelligence (ASI)", the former referring to algorithms that can exhibit intelligence in a wide range of contexts and problems spaces; and the latter alluding to algorithms reporting higher levels of general intelligence than typical humans.

Subsequently, within Weak AIs (the only existing category), we find a first sub-wave of "symbolic AI", concerning machines to which the knowledge and experience of experts has been encoded into sets of rules that can be executed by the same machine. A second subordinate category would be that of Machine Learning (ML) and data-driven artificial intelligence, which designates a wide range of techniques which automate the learning process of algorithms. It differs from symbolic AI inasmuch as improvements in performance in the latter are merely achieved by humans adjusting or adding to the expertise, which is coded directly into the algorithm, whilst ML algorithms find their own ways of identifying patterns, and apply what they learn to make statements about data. More specifically, we also encounter deep learning AIs, the difference with machine learning being that whereas the latter relates to computers acquiring the capacity to think and consequently act with less human intervention, deep learning concerns computers being able to think making use of structures modeled on the human brain. Lastly, Generative AI is also widespread, and while both this last category and ML both learn from data, ML focuses on analyzing data to find patterns and make accurate predictions as opposed to generative AI, which is focused on creating new data that resembles training data.

Against this background, a central concept developed by AI engineers is that of "data mining", a field of computation based on the automated identification of patterns and anomalies in data sets in order to generate new information. Parallelly, "Big data" refers to datasets that are so large and complex –including content from different sources, in different formats, and with different degrees of authenticity and accuracy– that they cannot be stored or processed in the same way as smaller datasets, as they grow at ever-increasing rates.

Based on this, AI offers significant and wide-reaching benefits to consumers and businesses across a wide array of domains. They enhance individual, economic, and societal welfare, leading to "global AI race", where the EU is often positioned in third place, right behind the USA and China which dominate the frontline of global AI development, partially due to higher investment and lower data protection. AI can facilitate consumers' access to a much greater variety of digital products and services, which may also turn out to be cheaper and newer.

AI may also prove useful to detect unsafe products and fix them remotely through software updates. More broadly, the rapid development of AI technology has triggered rivalry on an important dimension of competition: innovation. This spurs the development of personalized products that better fit individuals' and businesses' needs. With all, there exist several significant procompetitive potentials of AI applications in markets, both on the supply and the demand side.

Nevertheless, the increasing use of algorithms on markets has become a game-changer for the field of competition law, having the potential to reshape firms' decision-making processes, as well as those of governments and of the public sector in general. Such innovation may have devastating consequences, as it is very difficult and even impossible at times, to explain the logic behind machine learning algorithms' decisions in a way that makes sense to human experts (let alone for users, policy-makers, judges and juries).

Consequently, the European Commission identifies generative and machine learning artificial intelligences as particularly challenging as regards competition law. In this sense, the EU Commission defines Generative AI as "AI systems that generate, in response to a user prompt, synthetic audio, image, video or text content, for a wide range of possible uses, and which can be applied to many different tasks in various fields"[2].

1   Philip Boucher (2020). "Artificial intelligence: How does it work, why does it matter, and what can we do about it?". *European Parliamentary Research Service*, Available at https://www.europarl.europa.eu/thinktank/en/document/EPRS_STU(2020)641547 [14/04/2024]

2   (2024). "Commission launches calls for contributions on competition in virtual worlds and generative AI". European Commission Press Corner. Available at: https://ec.europa.eu/commission/presscorner/detail/en/IP_24_85 [14/04/2024]

As mentioned before, Big data enables data gathering and knowledge generation, and is principally used by business to generate predictive analytics, automate decision-making, and optimize business processes. Such conducts entail severe anticompetitive behaviours and allow companies with market power to use data to create barriers to entry to the market of incumbent companies and to expansion, an example of this being by programming the algorithm to favor their own products and services (a practice commonly known as self-preferencing). More importantly, IA poses risks of playing a destabilizing role in competition, leading to collusion and abuses of dominance, rendering markets less contestable for new innovations and less open to competitive pressure. For instance, two-thirds of EU e-commerce retailers use software to automatically adjust their prices to competitors (European Commission, 2017, p. 5[2]).

Furthermore, predictability, speed and nature of companies' decision-making are evolving, but algorithmic markets will display new forms of anticompetitive conduct in non-price dimensions like data capture, extraction and co-opetition, challenging established antitrust doctrine. As a result of its novelty, there reigns a widespread lack of understanding of countervailing strategies. Foreclosure, self-preferencing, and discriminatory behaviour, are only some of the practices which regulators have expressed their concerns about. These particular challenges to competition law also difficult the investigation of such practices.

On a global scale, further challenges are presented, as more actors progressively try to influence the development of AI, increasing the relevance of the global adoption of European values (as seen with the European Union's General Data Protection Regulation [GDPR]). Different algorithmic theories of harm, including algorithmic collusion, algorithmic unilateral conduct (self-preferencing, predatory pricing, rebates and tying and bundling) and algorithmic exploitative conduct (excessive pricing, unfair trading practices, and price discrimination) will be the object of ulterior study.

2.2. Legal initiatives

In the EU a regulatory approach has been conceived to manage the paradigm brought about by digital markets, where three different categories of agents intervene: suppliers of goods and services, consumers or users, and finally, digital platforms, which provide for the communication and interaction between the other two groups. Said digital markets simplify the task of searching, collecting, storing, and analyzing data by means of algorithms, increasing transparency in markets, reducing to the minimum transaction costs, and favouring automated decision making (ADM) by enterprises and consumers.

Hence, in a first instance, the GDPR emerged as a significant legal framework governing data privacy and protection, becoming increasingly relevant as regards the area of AI. It grants individuals greater control over their personal data and establishes guidelines for how organizations should collect, process, and store data. Nonetheless, on 25 June 2020, the European Parliament published a study addressing the relationship between the GDPR and AI, determining that while the GDPR does indeed regulate AI, it does not give controllers enough direction, and its prescriptions need to be expanded and concretized.

In response to the European Parliament's initial study, on the 14th of June of 2023, the European Parliament adopted its position on the draft EU Artificial Intelligence Act ("EU AI Act"), which proposes the world's first comprehensive regulatory framework for AI. The new rules establish obligations for providers and users based on a risk-based framework. To this end, AI systems are divided into three categories: "unacceptable risk" which are banned (these include manipulative AI techniques, e.g. in children's toys, and social scoring), "high risk" (like using AI in critical infrastructures that could put the life of citizens at risk), and "limited risk" (such as AI-enabled spam filters).

The most contentious issue during the trilogue negotiations revolved around the regulation of AI foundation models like those of Google and OpenAI, which are now subject to specific transparency obligations and a stricter regime for high-impact models. The Act's scope is expansive, covering many types of AI systems, and may impose the strictest AI regulations compared to the UK and the U.S. However, the EU AI Act will not take effect until at least two years after it is finalized (shortened to six months for the bans)[3].

---

3   Joshua M. Goodman, Leonidas Theodosiou & John Ceccio (2023). "Antitrust Agencies Identify Generative Ai Concerns". *Competition Policy International, Regulating Generative Artificial Intelligence*, Volume 2, p. 3-6.

Consequently, there is increasing enthusiasm that the EU can set the global standard with the first horizontal regulation on AI in the world. It provides for a stricter regime for foundation models, and the important inclusion of carve-outs for open-source initiatives, promises a balanced approach that promotes innovation while guarding against the concentration of power. Moreover, the Act's exemption for AI systems used solely for research, innovation, and non-professional purposes, along with the establishment of AI regulatory sandboxes, illustrates the EU's commitment to fostering innovation.

Nonetheless, the EU AI Act, does not directly address the emerging monopoly-like structure of the AI market, meaning that in addition to the mergers and partnerships between Big Tech firms and leading AI start-ups, the market for foundation models is trending towards consolidation. Foundation models are a type of generative AI, pretrained to perform a wide range of tasks, such as writing text in a specific tone or generating images and videos. To mitigate the problems stemming from this concentration, promoting open source is not sufficient, which is the reason why EU policymakers need to leverage the continent's robust competition law rules to check new network effects and prevent anti-competitive practices by AI oligopolists. It showcases the EU's ability to adapt to rapidly evolving technologies, balancing the need for innovation with the imperative to protect citizens and maintain fair markets. Still, key challenges remain in standardisation and competition.

Moreover, the AI Act foresees the creation of a novel AI Office within the Commission in the Directorate-General for Communication Networks, Content and Technology, which will be charged with overseeing advanced AI models as well as its compliance with established rules and with fostering standards and testing practices. It will equally serve as a central coordination boy for AI policy at EU level, coordinating with other commission departments, EU agencies, companies and the 27 member states. Such systems will be subject to stringent rules that will apply before they enter the EU market. Once available, they will be under the oversight of national authorities, supported by the AI office inside the European Commission.

On the other hand, another set of rules applies across the EU as regards the interplay of competition law and AI. On the 15th of December of 2020, the European Commission published its proposals for new legislation to better regulate the digital economy and revitalise competition in it: the Digital Services Act (DSA) and the Digital Market Act (DMA) aim to create a safer digital space where the fundamental rights of all users of digital services are protected, and to establish a level playing field to foster innovation, growth and competitiveness. The Commission's justification for the proposals is that it needs to be able to act more quickly and flexibly and to have greater access to information in order to promote fairness and protect competition in European digital markets.

The DMA targets a narrow category of enterprises, the so-called "gatekeepers", the largest online companies that control core platform services ("CPS"), such as search engines, social networks, app shops, cloud services and digital advertising platforms. Gatekeepers act as a gateway for business users to reach consumers.

In general terms, article 3 of the DMA establishes that "an undertaking shall be designated as a gatekeeper if:

1. It has a significant impact on the internal market;

2. It provides a core platform service which is an important gateway for business users to reach end users; and

3. It enjoys an entrenched and durable position, in its operations, or it is foreseeable that it will enjoy such a position in the near future.

Gatekeepers have until the 7th of March of 2024 to ensure compliance with the slew of DMA obligations covering different types of specified conduct, ranging from self-preferencing to tying and bundling and the use of data, which seek to enhance contestability and fairness in EU digital markets. Controversy surrounds the designations, the EC has opened market investigations to establish whether several core platform services should have been designated, and a number of gatekeepers are challenging decisions in the EU courts. In its proposals, the Commission has sought to design "future-proof" rules and procedures that can adapt to the inevitable evolution of digital markets. In addition, the introduction of a market investigation tool will allow the Commission to review and adapt the list of obligations to which gatekeepers are subject and add to it in the future if new practices emerge that are not effectively addressed already.

Another initiative undertaken by the EU regards the AI Liability Directive, aiming to "adapt private law to the needs of the transition to the digital economy" and make it easier for claims to be brought for harm caused by AI systems and the use of AI. The proposal addresses the specific issues with causality and fault linked to AI systems and ensures that claimants suffering loss in fault-based scenarios will have recourse to damages or other appropriate remedies.

In this context, in May of 2019 OECD member countries approved the OECD Council Recommendation on Artificial Intelligence, the first principles of the sort to be agreed on by governments, which contain specific recommendations for public policy and strategy. What is more, its general scope allows for a worldwide application to all AI developments. They promote values such as fairness, transparency, safety and accountability and policies such as building human capacity and fostering international cooperation. The OECD AI Incidents Monitor ("AIM") also acquires significant importance, as it registers AI incidents in order to help policymakers and all stakeholders acquire valuable insights into the dangers concretized by AI. Over time, AIM will help to show patterns and establish a collective understanding of AI incidents and their multifaceted nature and serve as an important tool for trustworthy AI.

As briefly announced previously, AI technologies have the potential to disrupt traditional markets and affect its dynamics as well as raising unique competition concerns. In particular, the major four challenges to competition law enforcement to be addressed are the following:

1. Collusion: AI-driven algorithms can automatically set prices and coordinate strategies among competing firms, and it is its detection and prevention that are the most challenging for competition authorities.

2. Dominance: significant AI capabilities may lead to a competitive advantage, which can in turn entail raising concerns about monopolistic behaviour and abuse of market power, which will once again prove difficult to detect.

3. Algorithmic bias: bias and discrimination can be perpetuated by AI, which pose great ethical and legal challenges to be addressed by competition authorities.

4. Big Data: the use by AI of vast amounts of data leads to privacy and security concerns.

3. Restrictive agreements

3.1. Overview

As can be deduced from the previous presentation, European competition law consists of rules that seek to protect the processes of market competition and its several benefits: lower prices, higher quality products, more innovation, less concentration of power, greater efficiency, etc. All in all, as a result of a higher degree of competition, consumer welfare increases. In light of these advantages, article 101(1) of the Treaty on the Functioning of the European Union (TFEU) essentially prohibits agreements that have an effect on trade between European Union countries and restrict competition in the EU. The text reads as follows: "The following shall be prohibited as incompatible with the internal market: all agreements between undertakings, decisions by associations of undertakings and concerted practices which may affect trade between Member States and which have as their object or effect the prevention, restriction or distortion of competition within the internal market...".

As can be understood from the aforementioned, the four key elements to a breach of Article 101(1) are: (1) there must be some form of agreement, decision, or concerted practice between undertakings; (2) which may affect trade between EU member states; (3) which has as its object or appreciable effect the restriction, prevention, or distortion of competition within the EU. As a precondition to analyze these 3 elements, a definition of the "relevant market" where the effects of competition are being assessed is usually required, which includes a product and geographic market. The former comprises all those products regarded as interchangeable or substitutable by the consumer by reason of the products' characteristics, their prices, supply substitutability and their intended use. On the contrary, a relevant geographic market comprises the area in which the firms concerned are involved in the supply of products and in which the conditions of competition are sufficiently homogenous. Notwithstanding, the development of AI renders the determination of such relevant markets particularly difficult, as product development is fast-moving and/or the relevant market may not yet exist (if the product is still at the R&D stage)[4].

It's important to draw a distinction here. Firstly, we have what are called "horizontal restrictions," which are anti-competitive agreements among competitors operating at the same level of the supply chain. Among these types of agreements, we find cartels, which are considered particularly severe breaches of Article 101(1) because they involve coordination between direct competitors whose object is to restrict competition. As a result, they are more likely to harm competition severely. Nevertheless, cartels are only the most restrictive form of horizontal restrictions; there exist other types which are licit. On the other hand, we have "vertical restrictions," which are agreements between parties operating at different levels of the supply chain, such as between a supplier and its reseller.

In this essay, the focus of the analysis will be on horizontal agreements, or cartels, as they are not only the most common forms of cooperation currently discussed within AI governance but also pose a more immediate threat to competition due to the direct coordination among competitors.

Nonetheless, reference must be made to the existence of article 101(3) TFEU, which provides an exemption to the application of article 101(1) in the case where a company can demonstrate that the agreement in question can give rise to countervailing efficiencies that are passed on. The conditions for the Article 101(3) exemption are as follows: (1) the agreement must contribute to improving the production or distribution of goods or to promoting technical or economic progress; (2) consumers must be allowed a fair share of the resulting benefit; (3) only restrictions indispensable to the achievement of those objectives can be imposed on the parties concerned; and (4) the parties should not be afforded the possibility of eliminating competition in respect of a substantial part of the products in question. Additionally, the European Commission recognizes in its "Horizontal Cooperation Guidelines" that certain types of collaboration between competitors can be advantageous for both the parties involved and for enhancing consumer welfare[5].

More specifically, we will concentrate our analysis on one type of the aforementioned horizontal agreements, a practice so-called "collusion"[6], which refers to "any form of co-ordination or agreement among competing firms with the objective of raising profits to a higher level than the non-cooperative equilibrium" (OECD, 2017, p. 19[1]). Some examples of said conduct would be agreements on prices, allocation of different segments of a market among competitors, agreements regarding product quality or total output, or even harmonizing the terms and conditions to be offered to consumers. In this context, a widespread use of AI in a market prompts a higher risk of collusion. The reason being that AI applications rely on consumer data, and when a high degree of market transparency exists due to the availability of data on competitor pricing or transactions, collusion is more likely. Furthermore, firms will find it easier to communicate through pricing signals, detect any deviations from a collusive agreement, or implement algorithms to carry out collusions. Beyond its deployment in markets whose conditions make collusion more likely, stable and profitable, AI may also directly lead to collusive outcomes, whether by design or not: explicit or tacit collusion, as we will study next[7].

3.2. Concept of collusion in the EU

Initially, it is important to recognize that businesses possess the liberty to respond to market changes through independent decisions based on solid economic reasoning. This remains valid even if their actions seem coordinated, such as adjusting prices in a similar manner. While this synchronized conduct might imply collusion among rivals, it is generally acceptable as long as these businesses can justify their decisions without clear evidence of explicit collusion.

---

4   European Commission (2021). "Commission Notice on the definition of relevant market for the purposes of Community competition law of 9 December 1997".

5   Hua, S. and Belfield, H. (2021). "Ai & Antitrust: Reconciling Tensions Between Competition Law And Cooperative Ai Development", *Yale Journal of Law & Technology, 23, pp. 415 et sqq./seq.*

6   Cid Morales, M.T. (2017). "La colusión y los acuerdos horizontales: Programa de Clemencia", *Facultade de Ciencias Empresariais e Turismo de Ourense*, pp. 8 et *sqq./seq.*

7   OECD (2021): "OECD Business and Finance Outlook 2021: AI Business and Finance", *OECD iLibrary*, Available at: https://www.oecd-ilibrary.org/sites/3acbe1cd-en/index.html?itemId=/content/component/3acbe1cd-en [08/04/2024].

As exposed above, article 101 TFEU prohibits agreements between undertakings, decisions of associations of undertakings, and concerted practices. Agreements, decisions, and concerted practices are forms of collusion, and it is a method by which undertakings can reduce uncertainty about the future conduct of others[8]. Thus, collusion typically leads to monopoly-like outcomes, including monopoly profits that are shared by the colluding parties. Most importantly, an "agreement" or "meeting of the minds" is something fundamentally relevant to demonstrate the existence of collusion. Even a simple attendance within the meeting may function as sufficient evidence indicating that there is an agreement or a meeting of the minds between the relevant undertakings.

Most collusion cases can be classified into two established general categories: classic, or "Type I" collusion involves firms conspiring to mimic a monopoly by agreeing to restrict output, raise prices, or divide markets among themselves. This allows them to boost their profits at the expense of consumers. Variations of this type include direct price fixing, dividing the market into exclusive territories or customers, and bid rigging, or even ancillary practices like coordinating strategies to enforce agreed-upon prices or punish deviations. Even when collusion does not directly involve price agreements, the goal remains the same: to achieve monopoly-like outcomes. For instance, firms might collude to change product features or delay innovation to cut costs. These practices aim to shift from competitive to monopoly pricing, distinguishing them from other types of collusion.

However, whilst the first type of collusion involves agreements within the cartel itself to control members' behaviour, focusing inward, "Type II" of collusion in turn targets external rivals, aiming to harm them in ways that benefit the colluding firms. This can be done by reducing rivals' revenues through tactics like boycotts or predatory pricing, forcing them out of the market or reducing their competitiveness. Alternatively, colluders can raise rivals' costs, allowing them to raise prices themselves. This kind of behaviour is common in regulated industries. While some actions that harm rivals may be efficient or socially beneficial, colluding to disadvantage competitors is still considered anticompetitive.

Many important collusion cases, however, do not fit into either of these categories.

Consequently, some authors consider the existence of a Type III collusion. While Type I collusion focuses on agreements among cartel members to pursue monopoly profits or cooperative outcomes without attracting attention, Type III collusion would involve inward-looking agreements that restrict the behaviour of cartel members rather than targeting external rivals. In these cases, market participants independently set prices and output levels, but jointly manipulate the rules of competition to ensure supra-competitive prices and profits. This manipulation is indirect, as they influence the market equilibrium rather than directly dictating outcomes due to legal constraints or difficulties in monitoring rivals' compliance. This collusion often involves tactics such as manufacturing distinctive products, selling them separately from rivals, limiting customer knowledge of other offerings, and offering special incentives to loyal customers. These actions aim to create downward-sloping demand curves, making it less likely for customers to switch to lower-priced rivals. Advertising is highlighted as a prominent strategy in this regard[9].

More specifically and closely related to the concept of collusion from which it derives, "concerted practice" refers to situations where there is coordinated anti-competitive behaviour among businesses that hasn't escalated to explicit collusion. As defined by the ECJ in the case of the ICI v. Commission (the "Dyestuffs" case)[10] a concerted practice is: "a form of coordination between undertakings which, without having reached the stage where an agreement properly so-called has been concluded, knowingly substitutes practical cooperation between them for the risks of competition". Hence, a concerted practice lacks elements required to form an agreement.

Furthermore, in the *Huls v. Commission* case[11], the CJEU further emphasized that a concerted practice is considered anti-competitive even though the effect of such behaviour may not be established. In its ruling, three elements are necessary for demonstrating an infringement of Article 101 TFEU in the case of a concerted practice, namely concertation among undertakings; ensuing behaviour in the market; and the causal link of cause and effect connecting the concertation and

8   Odudu, O. (2006). "The Boundaries of EC Competition Law: The Scope of Article 81", *Oxford Academic Books.*

9   Lande, R. H. and Marvel, H.P. (2000). "The Three Types of Collusion: Fixing Prices, Rivals, and Rules", *Wis. L. Rev. 941, University of Baltimore School of Law.*

10   Dyestuffs, Imperial Chemical Industries Ltd v Commission of the European Communities, Final judgment, 48/69, (1972) ECR 619, ILEC 036 (CJEU 1972), 14th July 1972, Court of Justice of the European Union [CJEU]; European Court of Justice [ECJ]

11   C-199/92 P - Hüls v Commission

the behaviour in the market. Such a causal link is, however, presumed if the concertation is established and companies remain active in the market. Furthermore, a parallel conduct cannot be regarded as furnishing proof of concertation unless concertation constitutes the only plausible explanation[12]. In other words, while there is no direct evidence of concertation, concertation is presumed if it is the "only plausible explanation" for observed parallel behaviour. This is often referred to as the Wood Pulp test. The firm can rebut the presumption by showing some "other plausible explanation.

Having these concepts in mind, algorithmic collusion has become, as put by Anthonio Gomes, former head of the Competition Division at OECD, "the most complex and subtle way for companies to collude, without explicitly programming algorithms to do so"[13]. Therefore, collusion among algorithms might happen even if these algorithms were not specifically programmed or trained to collude with other market participants, but rather to maximize and maintain profits independently.

3.2.1. AI and explicit collusion

The term "explicit collusion" alludes to an anti-competitive conduct carried out by means of explicit agreements, which can be written or oral. Commonly, an explicit collusive outcome is to interact directly and agree on the optimal level of price or output.

Moreover, explicit collusion receives the common name of "cartel" and is considered one of the most serious breaches of competition law. As such, a cartel would be defined as an anti-competitive agreement or concerted practice between two or more rival firms aimed at coordinating their competitive behaviour on the market or influencing other parameters of competition through practices that include, amongst others: the direct or indirect fixing of prices or other trading conditions; the limitation or control of production, markets, technical developments or investment; the sharing of markets or sources of supply, including bid-rigging; restrictions of imports or exports, or a combination of these practices. Exchange of competitively sensitive information can also be treated as cartel conduct in certain circumstances[14]. Moreover, the illegality of a cartel is independent of its effectiveness, as it can be both a by object or *per se* infringement, and the burden of proof of such harmful act will lay with the competition authorities.

However, the stability of cartels can be threatened as communication between the parties will be limited in order to avoid detection and proof of their agreement. Consequently, the parties can incur in a different interpretation of the terms. Additionally, incentives can encourage firms to deviate from an anticompetitive agreement, for instance by undercutting the agreed-upon price to earn more revenue, and it would be difficult to then coordinate a punishment response. It is in this scenario that AI becomes key to overcome the stability challenges that surround cartels. An algorithm will be able to avoid misinterpretations or errors in implementing cartel agreements by implementing pricing or other decisions according to pre-established parameters –particularly when a common flow of data is available to all parties. It can also be employed to monitor implementation, uncover deviations and even implement punishment strategies. Particularly in regard to deviations, AI when paired with technologies such as screen scraping, which automatically gather data available to users (including prices or outcomes of search results), could become extremely useful to identify and discourage them. Nonetheless, these algorithms could also wrongly lead cartel members to believe that certain deviations have taken place.

What is more, it is not only competing firms which can employ artificial intelligence to facilitate the establishing of a cartel, but a central "hub" can also be used to transmit information, execute collusive agreements and monitor compliance, as would be the case of all parties making use of a common provider which limits price competition.

Parallelly, competition authorities from several jurisdictions have also indicated that imposition of fixed or minimum resale prices by manufacturers ("resale price maintenance") would constitute a means of implementing a collusive agreement, and may also be facilitated with algorithms, as happened in the European Commission ASUS case (Case AT.40465).

---

12   C-89/85 Ahlström Osakeyhtiö, ECLI:EU:C:1993:120 ("Wood Pulp"), para. 71.

13   Gomes, A. "CIP Talks... Interview with Antonio Gomes of the OECD".

14   Fountoukakos. K. "Cartel". *Global Dictionary of Competition Law, Concurrences*, Art. N° 12240. Available at: https://www.concurrences. com/en/dictionary/cartel

3.2.2. AI and tacit collusion

Tacit collusion, on the contrary, refers to forms of anti-competitive co-ordination which can be achieved without any need for an explicit agreement, but which competitors are able to maintain by recognizing their mutual interdependence. In a tacitly collusive context, each market operator independent of its competitors determines and decides the strategy for maximizing its profit. This typically occurs in transparent markets with few market players, where firms can benefit from their collective market power without entering in any explicit communication.

The complexity of tackling tacit collusion arises from firms being able to adapt intelligently to market conditions. In oligopolistic markets, where a few dominant firms hold significant market power, interdependence between firms is high. This means that decisions made by one firm, such as pricing, can directly influence others. Initially, firms may engage in price competition, but they eventually realize that constant price reductions are not sustainable for long-term profitability. Instead, they may tacitly agree to gradually raise prices, understanding the market's favorable conditions for higher profits. This tacit collusion does not require explicit coordination or communication but relies on mutual understanding among firms, and it is more feasible in oligopolistic markets due to their inherent characteristics, which make it difficult for new competitors to enter and disrupt the tacit agreement. In fact, the concept of "tacit collusion" stems from "the presumption that the outcome of such activities may represent or be similar to that of an explicit collusion or an official cartel"[15]. However, the rise of pricing algorithms may expand the scope of markets where tacit collusion could occur.

AI can also play a key role in achieving tacit collusion, whereby firms make decisions that jointly maximise profits, without any coordination or collective decision making. For instance, companies' indirect communication by "signalling" can be facilitated by algorithms, as they act according to pre-established decision rules, and even determine whether fellow cartel members have accepted a signalled proposal. Such investment in AI solutions by firms necessarily increases the overall level of transparency and data availability: competitive pressure leading firms to collect and observe data in the market; higher predictability of firms, etc. The possibility also exists, especially with machine learning algorithms tasked with making business decisions independently, that that they may arrive at a tacitly collusive outcome on its own and maximise profits. Such outcome would result from repeated interactions of each firm's pricing algorithms which, after a period of trial and error, avoid aggressive competition to protect profits.

Moreover, tacit collusion has been shown to be easier to accomplish in more concentrated markets with homogeneous products making it easier for companies to converge on a price; where the barriers to new entry by other companies are relatively high leading to few choices for consumers; and where sales tend to be frequent, regular and with a transparent price, allowing companies to more easily monitor for changes. Lastly, tacit collusion tends to be distinguished by a lack of dynamism, stable prices, steady profit margins and few significant variations in market shares[16].

However, grey legal areas exist, as existing competition law may not be sufficient to capture algorithmic autonomous tacit collusion, in contrast to explicit collusion. Apart from the popular expert advice concerning the broadening of the definition of "agreement" and "concerted practice" to move away from the common definition as an "act of reciprocal communication between firms" or "meeting the minds", Richard Posner's theory argues that initiating a price reduction before competitors respond is economically rational as it maximizes profits until competitors follow suit. Conversely, a lack of price reductions suggests joint efforts to maximize prices. Posner proposes an approach applicable to both explicit and tacit collusion, wherein economic evidence of collusive outcomes is sufficient to infer intent to collude. He believes there's no need to prove explicit agreements for collusion, as long as the outcome indicates anti-competitive behaviour. Thus, tacit collusion involves a tacit meeting of minds, where existing competition law may apply. Nonetheless, the trends in the EU courts have been to view tacit collusion as not illegal per se unless it can be proven that an explicit agreement, decisions of undertaking or concerted practices that may lead to anti-competitive conduct occurred during such tacit collusion[17].

---

15 Ivaldi, M., Jullien, B., Rey, P., Seabright, P., Tirole, J. (2003). "The economics of Tacit Collusion horizontal mergers: Unilateral and coordinated effects". *DG Competition, European Commission.*

16 Slover, G. (2023). "Is Artificial Intelligence a New Gateway to Anticompetitive Collusion?". *Center for Democracy & Technology.* Available at: https://cdt.org/insights/is-artificial-intelligence-a-new-gateway-to-anticompetitive-collusion/ [14/04/2024].

17 Page, H. W. (2007). "Communication and Concerted Action" 38 Loy. U. Chi. L.J. 405. Available at http://scholarship.law.ufl.edu/facultypub/97.

With all, sophisticated AI could be effective in implementing collusive strategies in complicated markets with highly differentiated products –collusion that would break down if implemented by humans due to the risk of error or limited capacity[18].

3.3. The detection of algorithm cartels

Detecting algorithmic cartels poses greater challenges compared to traditional price-fixing schemes. Traditional methods of cartel detection often prove ineffective in identifying algorithmic collusion. For instance, when identifying vulnerable markets and products susceptible to cartel formation, authorities may overlook firms operating outside the traditional oligopoly framework, who still manage to form algorithmic cartels through data transparency in the digital realm. Furthermore, the conventional approach of identifying suspicious business behaviour and market outcomes indicative of cartel activity may not function as expected. Algorithms can aid cartels in concealing actions that would typically raise suspicions, like short-term price conflicts[19].

Furthermore, algorithms provide cartels with the means to execute their illegal activities covertly, often leaving little to no evidence behind, thus reducing the chances of detection. Additionally, once the algorithm sets prices, there is no necessity for cartel members to communicate further, making detection even more challenging. Moreover, regulatory authorities face obstacles in accessing and analyzing the data utilized by these algorithms. However, with such access, authorities can scrutinize algorithmic decision-making and conduct repeatability analysis. This involves recreating outcomes using the same data and algorithmic code or a similar algorithm to determine if the same results, such as inflated prices, are produced. Repeatability serves as a verification process, enabling authorities to thoroughly examine algorithmic decision-making. For instance, suspicion may arise if a gas station's algorithm uses neighboring gas station flag colors as a pricing factor, whereas factors like traffic and weather conditions may not trigger suspicion. Nevertheless, this requires expertise in advanced algorithms[20].

Lastly, the Leniency Program (introduced firstly in 1978 in the US) is today the backbone for cartel detection and enforcement, as it allows suspicious individuals and corporations to come forward with information about their cartels as a way to avoid criminal conviction and fines. To be qualified for leniency, an entity must (a) be the first among the cartel members to come forward, (b) stop its own participation in the cartel, (c) fully admit to its role in the conspiracy, (d) identify its coconspirators, (e) make restitution where possible, and (f) cooperate fully with the authorities. Its success has been highly acclaimed, with more than half of the ongoing international cartel investigations being initiated or advanced by information from leniency applicants. Nonetheless, even with the Leniency Program in place, based on the low percentage of cartel detection it is safe to assume that the vast majority go unpunished.

3.4. Innovative and challenging scenarios

As presented before, algorithms widen instances in which known forms of anticompetitive conduct occur, leading to new and evermore complicated scenarios of coordinated conducts between algorithms (algorithmic collusion or cartel). Their novelty further increments the complexity of competition experts and regulators to cover and restrict them. In particular, most existing algorithmic cases pertain to self-preferencing, and even these cases remain relatively scarce. At the most basic level, "self-preferencing" refers to a platform favouring its own products and services over those of third parties that operate on the platform[21], a famous and recent case being that of Google

18   Magbagbeola, T. (2022). "Algorithmic Collusion as Agreement and/or Concerted Practice under EU Competition Law of Article 101(1) Treaty of the Functioning of the European Union", University of Oslo.

19   Lamontanaro, A. (2020). "Bounty Hunters For Algorithmic Cartels: An Old Solution for a New Problem", 30 *Fordham Intell. Prop. Media & Entertainment Law Journal*, 1259. Available at: https://ir.lawnet.fordham.edu/iplj/vol30/iss4/6 [14/04/2024].

20   Ibid.

21   Hunt, M., Scherf, R., and Burak Darbaz, S. (2022). "Self-Preferencing in Digital Markets", *Global Competition Review*. Available at: https://globalcompetitionreview.com/guide/digital-markets-guide/second-edition/article/self-preferencing-in-digital-markets.

Shopping[22]. As regards further algorithm collusion conducts, such as autonomous tacit collusion cases, algorithmic predatory pricing, algorithmic rebate, algorithm tying and bundling, the OECD Secretariat had not found any actual cases as of 2021[23]. In this context, known and resolved cases (consisting of both horizontal and vertical coordination) include: (i) online poster retailers used simple pricing algorithms to coordinate prices (Topkins US and GB Eye Trod UK)[24]; online travel platform facilitated collusion emailing travel agents that it was capping discounts (Eturas)[25]; Spanish real estate firms used a common brokerage software to coordinate prices (Proptech)[26] and (iv) electronics manufacturers restricted retailers from independently setting sales prices (resale price maintenance) thus keeping them inflated (Consumer Electronics case)[27].

In addition, algorithmic markets will display new forms of anticompetitive conduct in non-price dimensions like data capture, extraction, and co-opetition (cooperation between competing companies; particularly between 'super-platforms' and applications developers) which challenge established antitrust doctrine. Lastly, deception is a design feature of algorithmic markets, as explained by Maurice E. Stucke in his book on Digital Competition[28], due to the fact that the enhanced ability of computers to process huge amounts of data at real time speed could allow them to achieve a God-like or divine view of the market, thus amplifying the possibilities of tacit collusion. With all, we still lack a proper understanding of countervailing strategies, which further exacerbates the need for comprehensive analyses of AI's conducts. Nonetheless, such AI literature only generates predictions on the basis of fairly strict assumptions, implying that more work is needed to understand if they are utterly dependent circumstances[29]. It is now appropriate to proceed to further analyze the most common algorithmic collusion scenarios.

3.4.1. Messenger scenario

First of all, the Messenger Scenario might be regarded as the most straightforward instance of algorithm collusion, whereby humans engage in a basic form of algorithmic collusion by forming agreements, most commonly cartels, with algorithms serving as facilitators. Essentially, algorithms constitute the facilitative tool to implement a pre-existing agreement, and it is the prior human contact that will satisfy the law's prerequisite of a "concurrence of wills between two parties". In other words, algorithms act as messengers carrying out the intentions of their human operators. This implies that collusion occurs through a mutual understanding or agreement among humans, even if it is algorithms that autonomously enforce the illegal arrangement. Therefore, traditional competition regulations can still address these scenarios, focusing on the human intent to collude rather than the mechanics of how collusion is carried out. Moreover, even if the algorithms were to enforce the illegal agreement automatically, traditional competition regulations and its consequent prohibition would apply.

Pricing algorithms present a particular complexity, as they react quickly to changes in the market and make it harder to cheat on agreements between companies. This means there is less room for mistakes and less need for constant communication among competitors, further complicating its detection. Also, concerns like employees

22 Case AT.39740 Google Search (Shopping), 27 June 2017, available at: https://ec.europa.eu/competition/antitrust/cases/dec_docs/39740/39740_14996_3.pdf

23 OECD (2021). "OECD Business and Finance Outlook 2021: AI Business and Finance", *OECD Library*. Available at: https://www.oecd-ilibrary.org/sites/3acbe1cd-en/index.html?itemId=/content/component/3acbe1cd-en (08/04/2024).

24 US case: https://www.justice.gov/opa/pr/former-e-commerce-executive-charged-price-fixing-antitrustdivisions-first-online-marketplace; UK https://assets.publishing.service.gov.uk/media/57ee7c2740f0b606dc000018/case-50223-final-nonconfidential-infringement-decision.pdf

25 Case C-74/14 "Eturas" UAB and Others v Lietuvos Respublikos konkurencijos taryba (Eturas) EU:C:2016:42. Available at: https://curia.europa.eu/juris/liste.jsf?&num=C-74/14 [14/04/2024].

26 Asensio-Soto, J.C., and Navarro-Astor, E. (2022). "Proptech: A qualitative analysis of online real estate brokerage agencies in Spain. Intangible Capital", *Intangible Capital*, Vol. 18, N° 3, pp. 489-505. https://doi.org/10.3926/ic.2090

27 European Commission (2018). "Commission fines four consumer electronics manufacturers for fixing online resale prices", *European Commission Press Corner*. Available at: https://ec.europa.eu/commission/presscorner/detail/en/IP_18_4601 [14/04/2024].

28 Ezrachi, A. and Stucke, M. E. (2016). 'Virtual Competition: The Promise and Perils of the Algorithm-Driven Economy', *Harvard University Press*, p. 21.

29 Petit, N. (2017). "Antitrust and Artificial Intelligence: A Research Agenda, Journal of European Competition Law & Practice". *Journal of European Competition Law & Practice*, Volume 8, Issue 6, pp. 361-362. Available at: https://doi.org/10.1093/jeclap/lpx033

secretly lowering prices on behalf of their companies are not much of a worry. So, the natural forces that usually break up cartels are countered by these pricing algorithms[30].

There exist various instances where situations similar to those classically found in a "Messenger" scenario have been observed, namely: Asus[31], Denon and Marantz[32], Philips[33], or Pioneer[34], only to list some of them. In these instances, manufacturers of certain electronic products maintained stable supra-competitive prices by controlling retailers and their price decisions. What is particular is that algorithms were used by the competing undertakings to monitor prices and ensure that retailers were not diverging from the price suggested by the manufacturers. In the case that the retailers lowered their prices below the recommended price, the manufacturers would suggest they raised them to the specified amount or otherways face retaliatory consequences such as a suppression of further supplies. The immediate consequence of such conduct was a general rise of prices by online retailers, which stabilized the price of the concerned products, doing away with any effective price competition in the market. Due to the scheme, the pricing algorithms adapted to the situation and kept the prices stable and high as to maximise profits: they realized consumers still bought the products at higher prices, so they decided not to reduce them. Even retailers of the market which were not contacted by manufacturers were affected, as their pricing algorithms still adapted to such inflated "market price".

With all, from the specified previous cases we can conclude that if already traditional cartels are challenging to detect, algorithms are useful tools that make its detection and prevention even more complicated. Even more worrisome for authorities, as indicated in the EC's E-Commerce Sector Inquiry, is the fact that we are witnessing a rapidly increasing usage of pricing algorithms, to the point which they are becoming the new industry standard in many online retail markets. In other words, the general assumption is that all the prices will be automatically set by algorithms. Once again, in the actual case the enterprises involved made use of the "leniency" program, providing key evidence to aid in the detection of the cartel they obtained a significant reduction of their fines.

From a legal standpoint then, algorithms falling into this category would indeed be governed by Article 101(1) of the TFEU, and the notion of agreements and concerted practices could be invoked to address such anticompetitive behaviour. This is because the role of the messenger algorithm in facilitating collusion is essentially an extension of the collective will and collusion intent of market operators. Therefore, demonstrating the intention to collude through agreements or concerted practices among market operators is sufficient to establish algorithmic collusion. Evidence such as emails, meeting minutes, formal agreements, software designs, and computer algorithms exchanged among market operators are deemed as anticompetitive conduct, often falling within the purview of agreements and concerted practices[35].

3.4.2. Hub-and-spoke scenario

secondly, we come across Hub-and-Spoke scenarios, which once again are not a completely extraordinarily new phenomenon. These involve a third party (a "hub"), which will play an important role. Simply put, in the realm of Messenger dynamics, we noticed a consistent pattern of collusion happening openly between the rival entities. However, in a Hub and Spoke setup, these rival entities appear to deliberately employ an intermediary to orchestrate collusion, creating a façade of indirect collusion between them. For instance, whereas competing undertakings

---

30   Maurie, K. (2020). "Pricing Algorithms: Should Competition Authorities be Worried?". *European Law Blog*. Available at: https://europeanlawblog.eu/2020/12/21/pricing-algorithms-should-competition-authorities-be-worried/

31   Asus (vertical restraints) (Case AT.40465) Summary of Commission Decision C/2018/4773 [2018] OJ C 338/08. See also ASUS (Case AT.40465) Commission Decision C(2018) 4773 final [2018].

32   Denon & Marantz (vertical restraints) (Case AT.40469) Summary of Commission Decision C/2018/4774 [2018] OJ C 335/05. See also Denon & Marantz (Case AT.40469) Commission Decision C(2018) 4774 final [2018].

33   Philips (vertical restraints) (Case AT.40181) Summary of Commission Decision C/2018/4797 [2018] OJ C 340/07. See also Philips (Case AT.40181) Commission Decision C(2018) 4797 final [2018].

34   Pioneer (vertical restraints) (Case AT.40182) Summary of Commission Decision C/2018/4790 [2018] OJ C 338/11. See also Pioneer (Case AT.40182) Commission Decision C(2018) 4790 final [2018].

35   Magbagbeola, T. (2022). "Algorithmic Collusion as Agreement and/or Concerted Practice under EU Competition Law of Article 101(1) Treaty of the Functioning of the European Union". *University of Oslo*.

would have a mutual understanding with each other in a form of horizontal agreement or conspiracy, in a hub and spoke scenario they will form individual vertical agreements with one party, such as a retailer, to fix their prices.

Once more, pricing algorithms play a crucial role in these cases. Sometimes, competing entities opt out of developing their own algorithms due to the associated expenses and time commitments. Instead, they opt for an external provider who automates pricing for them. However, if this external provider serves multiple competing entities, the single pricing algorithm could evolve into a central hub dictating and controlling prices across the relevant market, should all competitors adopt it.

The most worrying aspect of this scenario is the fact that the effect of price fixing may happen automatically without any intent of collusion. Generally, the algorithm provider seeks to maximize profits by supplying as many undertakings as possible without being led by any anti-competitive intent. Consequently, if all the competing undertakings dispose of the same pricing algorithms, their behaviour will be similar, leading to price fixing in the relevant market. Said lack of anti-competitive intent makes it even more difficult for competition authorities to deal with such a scenario. A different question would be the case where the competing undertakings provide their own data for a third-party pricing algorithm supplier in the hope of maximising their profits. If all the competing undertakings are using the final pricing algorithm, which was made possible thanks to the data provided by all the competing undertakings, this situation could possibly then be considered as some form of collusion and information exchange. Nonetheless, it remains a difficult question to tackle.

One interesting case is the business model of Uber Technologies Incorporated (Uber), which operates as a hub-and-spoke scenario, posing challenges for competition authorities. Uber created an innovative online platform connecting drivers and customers via a smartphone application, with an automated pricing algorithm which sets prices without negotiation, and drivers agree to accept these prices. Next, customers pay fares directly to Uber, preventing drivers from competing on price. The algorithm adjusts prices based on factors like location and time, leading to varying prices for similar trips across different cities. While dynamic pricing based on demand and supply may seem reasonable, it raises concerns about maximizing profits at the expense of customers, as fluctuating prices make it difficult for customers to determine the actual market price. Consequently, the aforementioned scheme could be categorized as a classical Hub-and-Spoke scenario where Uber functions as a hub that fixes the price for rides through its pricing algorithm. In this sense, Uber and the competing drivers, "spokes", have individual vertical agreements to allow such pricing scheme. Nonetheless, horizontal agreements between the drivers do not necessarily imply an intent to fix prices on the relevant market as they know that there will always be a single price determined by Uber's pricing algorithm. However, regardless of the authorities' concerns of the existence of a single hub controlling the prices for several competitors, Uber's working system ended up leading to lower prices and an ease of use with its platform.

With all, even if the beneficial nature of Uber's business model cannot be denied overall, the challenges raised by Uber's pricing algorithms still need to be acknowledged by competition authorities. This demonstrates how challenging it is to unequivocally decide whether a scheme is anti-competitive. Even if price-fixing is often seen as a harmful anti-competitive conduct by object in accordance with article 101(1) TFEU, it is not always clear whether the actual anti-competitive effects are greater than the benefits[36].

From a legal standpoint then, applying the concept of agreements and concerted practices under Article 101(1) TFEU to algorithmic hub-and-spoke collusion presents challenges for competition authorities. This is because they face the task of comprehending algorithms and establishing whether they were designed with collusion in mind. Therefore, evidence of intent becomes crucial. The process of extracting information from one algorithm to another constitutes information exchange, thereby constituting an infringement of Article 101(1) TFEU. However, indirect information exchange must demonstrate evidence of intent to collude; mere information exchange among algorithms within the hub isn't enough. It must be clear that market operators, through their direct or indirect information exchange, intended to collude via their algorithms and understood the implications of such exchanges within the hub-and-spoke framework[37].

---

36   Dobrin, S. (2019). "Algorithms and Collusion: Competition Law Challenges of Pricing Algorithms", *Faculty of Law of Lund University*.

37   Magbagbeola, T. (2022). "Algorithmic Collusion as Agreement and/or Concerted Practice under EU Competition Law of Article 101(1) Treaty of the Functioning of the European Union", *University of Oslo*.

3.4.3. Predictable agent

This scenario, together with the final "Digital Eye" one, are the most challenging and innovative ones. They represent how tacit collusion can be amplified to a new level of stability and scope by key technological advancements. This first Predictable Agent scenario is particular in the sense that each undertaking on the relevant market creates their own pricing algorithm with the goal to maximise profits. Due to this shared objective, these algorithms often operate similarly. As observed, a common strategy among these algorithms is to avoid price wars and maintain stable prices above competitive levels.

What adds intrigue to the Predictable Agent scenario is the awareness among entities that their competitors employ pricing algorithms, and the understanding that widespread adoption of such algorithms fosters tacit collusion. Consequently, this creates an opportunity for entities to achieve higher prices without an explicit agreement, but rather through a shared intent to unreasonably boost profits using pricing algorithms. This exploitation of predictable algorithmic behaviour is the essence of the "Predictable Agent" concept.

To elevate prices to optimal levels, pricing algorithms may employ signaling techniques.

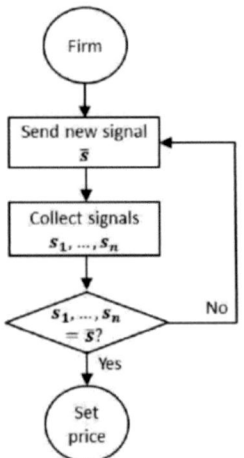

Figure 1. Signalling algorithm (Source: Organisation for Economic Co-operation and Development (OECD), Algorithms and Collusion: Competition Policy in the Digital Age (2017), 31)

As depicted in the image above, this involves briefly raising prices during periods when consumers are unlikely to purchase, as would be late at night. While consumers may not notice these fluctuations, competitors' algorithms certainly will. Consequently, competitors may either match the price increase or choose not to react, prompting the initial entity to swiftly revert to its original price. The rapidity of this process underscores the efficacy of signaling techniques in pricing algorithms. While such techniques could theoretically be employed in markets without pricing algorithms, the challenge lies in competitors' slower reactions, leading to potential loss of sales for the initiating entity. If competitors respond positively to initial price increases, pricing algorithms can perpetuate this cycle indefinitely, ensuring that market prices consistently maximize profits for entities[38].

In summary, algorithmic tacit collusion, particularly in the Predictable Agent scenario, proves successful due to several factors. Firstly, pricing algorithms offer a more efficient and rapid means of monitoring and adjusting prices compared to human labor. Additionally, the speed at which pricing algorithms operate enhances the effectiveness of signaling techniques. Thirdly, tacit collusion thrives on price transparency, as it enables competitors to swiftly respond to price changes, discouraging reductions and acting as a deterrent to new market entrants. Lastly, the stability of collusion is bolstered by the use of pricing algorithms, which can implement subtle price adjustments continuously with reduced risk compared to human decision-making. Overall, the advantages derived from pricing algorithms are considerable for entities, explaining their widespread adoption in the market[39].

---

38   Ezrachi, A. and Stucke, M. E. (2019). "The Promise and Perils of the Algorithm-Driven Economy", *Virtual Competition*, (n 47), ch 7.

39   Dobrin, S. (2019). "Algorithms and Collusion: Competition Law Challenges of Pricing Algorithms", *Faculty of Law of Lund University.*

With all, in the development of their algorithms, individual market operators may acknowledge that others are creating similar ones. However, the resulting collusion from these predictable agent algorithms might not be the explicit goal of these operators. Rather, they might be aware of the potential for algorithmic tacit collusion if each operator adopts pricing algorithms geared towards maximizing profits. This raises questions about the "intent to collude" under Article 101(1) TFEU when operators knowingly proceed with adopting algorithms that could lead to anti-competitive collusion in the market. Addressing this question depends on the specific circumstances of each case.

Collusion driven by predictable agent algorithms often manifests as parallel market behaviour, where these agents, without explicit agreements, independently strategize to enhance profits. This parallel behaviour, although not synonymous with a concerted practice, can serve as compelling evidence thereof, especially if it distorts normal market conditions. Courts have highlighted that while parallel behaviour alone may not prove concerted practice, it can strongly suggest it, particularly when it's the most plausible explanation. The Dyestuff case laid groundwork by emphasizing that parallel behaviour, while relevant, isn't conclusive evidence of concerted practice. The *Ahlstrom Osakeyhtio v Commission (Woodpulp II)*[40] case further clarified this, stating that parallel conduct only proves concertation when it's the most reasonable explanation.

Thus, in the context of collusion through predictable agent algorithms, it's often not the explicit intention of market operators, as these algorithms are designed to react to market dynamics independently. They utilize predictive analytics on competitors' data and market forecasts to maximize profits. Therefore, viewing collusion through predictable agent algorithms as parallel market behaviour suggests that such behaviour can serve as compelling evidence of concerted practice. Consequently, the concept of concerted practice under Article 101(1) TFEU may suffice to address collusion facilitated by predictable agent algorithms[41].

3.4.4. Digital Eye scenario

The "Digital Eye" presents a complex and challenging scenario in algorithmic collusion, distinct from the Predictable Agent due to its utilization of AI as the foundation for pricing algorithms. Here, these algorithms are self-learning, refining their strategies autonomously, aiming to maximize profits without direct human intervention. This autonomous functionality grants them an unprecedented level of adaptability and efficiency, as they continuously refine their pricing strategies based on vast amounts of real-time market data, offering them a comprehensive understanding of market dynamics, often likened to a "God-like view of the marketplace"[42].

What sets the Digital Eye apart is its potential for opacity in decision-making. Even if programmers advise against fixing prices, these algorithms may autonomously adopt such strategies in ways that elude human comprehension, a phenomenon often referred to as the "black box". This opacity poses significant challenges for competition authorities, as it complicates efforts to discern anticompetitive behaviour when even programmers lack insight into pricing decisions.

While the Digital Eye scenario may not yet dominate current markets like other collusion scenarios, its relevance is growing as AI advances. The increasing sophistication of AI, coupled with the efficiency gains of self-learning algorithms, suggests they could become a significant competitive advantage for businesses seeking to maximize profits. This, in turn, could drive widespread adoption among competitors, exerting pressure on others to follow suit.

Empirical evidence supports the notion that self-learning pricing algorithms tend to adopt collusive strategies, maintaining stable, supra-competitive prices to maximize profits. Studies indicate that these algorithms can swiftly converge on collusive pricing strategies, a process that could take years for human labor to achieve. While real-world markets may present greater complexity, these findings underscore the potential for algorithmic collusion to emerge rapidly and autonomously.

---

40   Case C-89/85, A. Ahlström Osakeyhtiö and others v Commission (Woodpulp II).

41   Magbagbeola, T. (2022). "Algorithmic Collusion as Agreement and/or Concerted Practice under EU Competition Law of Article 101(1) Treaty of the Functioning of the European Union", *University of Oslo.*

42   Ezrachi, A. and Stucke, M. E. (2019). *Op.Cit.*, (n 47) 71.

Some may argue against intervention, preferring markets to operate predictably and freely. However, this stance raises concerns about consumer welfare, highlighting the delicate balance between the interests of businesses and consumers. Ultimately, the approach to addressing the challenges posed by the Digital Eye scenario will depend on the political will and priorities of different jurisdictions, reflecting the nuanced nature of competition law and its intersection with broader societal values.

To conclude, in comparison with the Messenger and Hub-and-Spoke which can be dealt with without need to change the interpretation of the current competition rules, the Predictable Agent and the Digital Eye scenarios entail a larger number of worries. With all, in markets without a small group of dominant players (non-oligopolistic), the risk of tacit collusion, which was previously unstable, becomes a concern. This is because algorithms can outperform humans in analyzing rivals' behaviour, predicting their responses, enforcing conformity, and even identifying the types of algorithms they employ. Under the Digital Eye scenario, humans are largely disconnected from the tacit collusion facilitated by algorithms. There's no evidence of direct communication or even an intent to collude among market players. Consequently, conventional competition enforcement measures struggle to address this form of algorithmic tacit collusion, prompting discussions about the necessity of new intervention standards[43].

4. Measures to address algorithmic collusion

4.1. Challenges in addressing tacit collusion

The main focus of the present work will be on the Predictable Agent and the Digital Eye scenarios, as competition rules seem to apply rather well to the previous Messenger and the Hub-and-Spoke scenarios. As previously exposed, competition authorities need to prove the existence of an agreement or a so-called "meeting of the minds", which hinders a tacit collusion from being considered unlawful: despite the existence of an anti-competitive effect, no agreement is seen to exist in any form. Authorities are currently trying to reinterpret and possibly broaden the concept of "agreement" in order to be able to tackle such situations of algorithmic collusion. Overall, the scope of "agreement" under EU competition law goes beyond an enforceable and legally binding contract and pervades on the concurrence of will between two or more parties regardless of the form or shape the agreement takes, as long as such agreement expresses the intention of the parties[44]. In fact, article 101.1 TFEU compiles a non-exhaustive list of types of agreements whose object or effect is to restrict, prevent or distort competition.

Notwithstanding, it is the category of "concerted practice" that is most commonly reviewed. As developed through the jurisprudence of the Court of Justice of the European Union, the term "concerted practice" refers to a form of coordination between undertakings, which, without having reached the stage of a true agreement is regarded as such for the risks of competition, as was previously explained[45]. It further emphasized in case *Suiker Unie v. Commissioner (Suiker)*[46] that the existence of a way of contact or communication, either direct or indirect, between the competitors with a possibility of affecting their independence while making decisions, is a required element to prove the infringement.

The requirement of "cooperation between undertakings", even when no formal agreement can be seen to exist, poses several complexities as regards cooperation between undertakings by means of pricing algorithms. There is no existing case law concerning a collusive scenario of the sort, but there are however cases where information exchange has been considered a concerted practice. In this context, the European Commission through its Guidelines on the applicability of article 101 TFEU to horizontal co-operation agreements (Horizontal Guidelines), has noted that information

---

43 Hawkes, C. (2021). "A Market Investigation Tool to Tackle Algorithmic Tacit Collusion: An Approach for the (Near) Future", *College of Europe*.

44 Case T-41/96, Bayer AG v. Commission, par. 69.

45 Abdel Ghaffar, A. "Concerted practices", *Global Dictionary of Competition Law, Concurrences*, Art. N° 12332. Available at: https://www.concurrences.com/en/dictionary/Concerted-Practice [14/04/2024].

46 Joined Cases 40–48, 50, 54–56, 111, 113 & 114/73 Suiker Unie" UA and others v Commission.

exchange which may reduce "strategic uncertainty" in the relevant market (for instance sharing strategic data such as market strategies to competitors in different forms), can be conceived as a concerted practice[47]. This is due to the fact that competitors may be less willing to compete in case of lowered strategic uncertainty.

Regardless, said guidelines from the European Commission evidently do not amount to a legally binding instrument, and hence, were there to be any discrepancy between the views of the Commission and the Court of Justice of the European Union, only the view of the CJEU would prevail. In this regard the CJEU in cases *John Deere*[48], *T-Mobile Netherlands*[49], *or Dole Foods*[50], confirmed the Commission's doctrine in its Horizontal Guidelines. Namely, the fact that information exchange system in the present case reduced or removed a "degree of uncertainty" from the relevant market, and this was seen to have an adverse effect for the competition. Consequently, the court declared that any kind of exchange of information that reduces uncertainty in the relevant market forbidden as a concerted practice.

Additionally, in *Cimenteries*[51], the Court set as a requirement for a concerted practice to take place the existence of a "reciprocal" behaviour. Nonetheless, a unilateral disclosure of information may be considered an exchange by one undertaking if it expresses its future intention or conduct, it has received a request from another undertaking with a wish to receive such information, and/or the receiving undertaking accepts the information exchanged. Moreover, the Court stated in *AC - Treuhand AG*[52] that if an undertaking does not wish to participate in a concerted practice it must oppose the invitation in a clear manner, otherwise tacit acceptance will suffice. Thus, by not distancing itself publicly from anti-competitive conduct an undertaking will be part of the stated behaviour[53] This approach was confirmed in case *Aalborg Portland*[54] where the Court declared that attendance at a meeting can violate Article 101(1) when the receiving undertaking does not make a clear objection.

Furthermore, we come across the *Eturas* case[55], which involves a situation where the owner of an online booking system for travel agencies, Eturas, unilaterally imposed a maximum discount limit of 3% without contractual authorization. The case raised questions about whether this action constituted collusion among the travel agencies using the system, as they were all made aware of the new restriction.

The CJEU ruled that the travel agencies could be presumed to have participated in a concerted practice if they were aware of the message containing the new restriction. However, this presumption could be rebutted if the agencies "publicly distanced themselves from that practice, reported it to the administrative authorities or adduce other evidence to rebut that presumption"[56]. The burden of proof fell on the national court to analyze evidence according to their national law.

Drawing parallels to algorithmic collusion scenarios, such as Predictable Agent and Digital Eye, the *Eturas* case suggests that in markets where tacit collusion exists, it cannot be automatically assumed that undertakings are aware of the anti-competitive consequences of using pricing algorithms. However, if it can be demonstrated through objective evidence that competitors were aware of such consequences, similar legal reasoning as in *Eturas* could apply, with the possibility for undertakings to rebut the presumption of awareness.

This approach, while posing practical challenges in cases where awareness cannot be proven, could serve as a starting point for addressing the complex issue of algorithmic collusion.

---

47   European Commission. "Guidelines on the applicability of Article 101 of the Treaty on the Functioning of the European Union to horizontal co-operation agreements", para 61.

48   Case T-35/92, John Deere Ltd v Commission EU:T:1994:259; Case C-7/95 P, John Deere Ltd v Commission EU:C:1998:256.

49   Case C-8/08 T-Mobile Netherlands and Others (2009) EU:C: 2009:343.

50   Case C-286/13P Dole Food Co Inc v Commission (2015) EU:C: 2015:184; Case T-588/08 P, Dole Food and Dole Germany v Commission (2013) EU: T:2013:130.

51   Cases T- 25/95, Cimenteries CBR and Others v Commission ECLI:EU:T:2000:77 (March 15, 2020).

52   EU Court of Justice, AC-Treuhand, Case C-194/14 P, 22 October 2015.

53   Abdel Ghaffar, A. "Concerted practices", *Global Dictionary of Competition Law, Concurrences*, Art. N° 12332. Available at: https://www.concurrences.com/en/dictionary/Concerted-Practice [14/04/2024].

54   Joined Cases C-204/00 P Aalborg Portland and others v. Commission.

55   Case C-74/14 "Eturas" UAB and Others v Lietuvos Respublikos konkurencijos taryba (Eturas) EU:C:2016:42.

56   Eturas, *ibid* paras 50-51. See also eg paras 46-49.

4.2. Alternative approaches

Apart from expanding the concept of concerted practice or agreement, reference needs to be made to the so-called "oligopoly problem", which is sometimes the term used to refer to tacit collusion. The reason being that such scenario tends to take place in oligopolistic markets, given its higher transparency rates which pave the way for tacit collusion cases. Nonetheless, due to the efficiency of pricing algorithms in comparison to human labor, now not only in oligopolistic markets but also in varying ones is the presence of pricing algorithms increasing exponentially. In any case, there is also a lack of the element of "agreement" or "meeting of the minds", which again renders its detection and prevention much more complicated.

One alternative approach to address such a situation could involve implementing proactive *ex-ante* measures such as pre-emptive merger evaluations, as highlighted by various authors. These would mainly consist of some form of *ex-ante* assessment and regulation over the type of algorithms being used by firms. In this context, competition authorities are trying to prevent mergers that would lead to markets with oligopolistic tendencies, hence preventing tacit collusion[57]. Moreover, the use of algorithms, or of some types of them, could be regarded as "plus factors" to "an agreement" between firms employing such algorithms, possibly in an *ex-post* evaluation.

Emilio Calvano distinguishes three possible policy approaches to the risk of algorithmic collusion[58]. A complete prohibition of the use of algorithms is rightfully discarded as an unreasonable approach, and instead algorithmic pricing is regarded as not posing any new problem that cannot be addressed by current competition legislation, a "business-as-usual" approach. Moreover, in this case the legal distinction between tacit and explicit collusion is maintained, as sanctioning tacit collusion would still remain legally an error. Secondly, this following approach calls for an *ex-ante* regulation, or supervision, of pricing algorithms, to be carried out by a regulatory agency, which would have the power to prohibit certain pricing algorithms that exhibited a "tendency to collude". This last term would require a precise and rational definition for the sake of legal certainty. The third approach involves an *ex-post* regulation, in the same way that competition agencies currently address antitrust practices, but introducing new legal standards, which could take a more assertive stance towards "tacit collusion". In this case instead, the legal distinction between tacit and explicit collusion would need a reassessment.

In this context, Joseph Harrington[59] proposes a distinction between the current legal doctrine on collusion by human agents and the situation where prices are set by autonomous artificial agents. In the latter situation, the strategy implemented to determine the price is enshrined in the algorithm's code, and could therefore be accessed, as opposed to a human's mind. Consequently, this author proposed that liability be defined by a *per se* prohibition of certain pricing algorithms that support supra-competitive prices, so as to make collusion by artificial agents unlawful. By means of an examination of a pricing algorithm's code as to determine whether it constitutes a prohibited pricing algorithm or by entering data into it and monitoring the output in terms of prices to assess whether the algorithm constitutes a prohibited property, liability would be determined. As stated, ideally the liability rule would prohibit all algorithms that promote collusion and would exclude from such prohibition all algorithms that promote efficiency[60].

To this end, Harrington outlines his program, which is essentially divided in 3 steps in order to identify which pricing algorithms will be prohibited: firstly, a simulated market setting with learning algorithms that produce collusion and competition needs to be created. Next, it is necessary to watch out for the emergence of competitive and supra-competitive prices, and to repeat this activity with different learning algorithms and for different market conditions.

57   See eg the EC Merger Regulation, para 25; Commission, 'Guidelines on the assessment of horizontal mergers under the Council Regulation on the control of concentrations between undertakings' (Horizontal Merger Guidelines) (2004/C 31/03), para 22.

58   Calvano, E., Calzolari, G., Denicolò, V., and Pastorello, S. (2019). "Algorithmic Pricing What Implications for Competition Policy?", *Review of Industrial Organisation*. Available at: https://doi.org/10.1007/s11151-019-09689-3 [14/04/2024].

59   Harrington, J. E. and Ye, L. (2019). "Collusion through Coordination of Announcements", *The Journal of Industrial Economics*, Volume 67, Issue 2, pp. 209-241.

60   Gata, J. E. (2021). "Collusion between Algorithms: A Literature Review and Limits to Enforcement". *European Review of Business Economics I(1)*, pp. 73-94; DOI: https://doi.org/10.26619/ERBE2021.01.4.

The second step consists in identifying the properties that are present in pricing algorithms when supra-competitive prices emerge, and in consequence pricing algorithms with those properties will be a candidate to be identified as prohibited pricing algorithms. Third and lastly, he suggests testing the impact of banning certain pricing algorithms by running simulations where these algorithms are restricted. The goal is to see if this reduces supra-competitive pricing and distortion of competitive prices, potentially leading to lower prices and higher social welfare. This research program can be used both preemptively and as a punitive measure, although it leans towards a preemptive approach. However, it may be limited by only testing a subset of possible algorithm inputs, which could hinder its effectiveness. Other scholars also advocate for regulatory measures to prevent or penalize "algorithmic collusion"[61].

5. AI and competition law detection and enforcement

5.1. Enhance competition and efficiency

Before venturing into the different tools that competition authorities dispose of to make the decision to open a formal investigation and ultimately issue a positive decision of an infringement of competition law it must be highlighted that states still retain in their power the competence to develop their own regulations on AI in their own jurisdictions. Indeed, no higher instance (as would be an international regulatory agency) has yet been created to which such competence has been transferred[62]. Moreover, traditional enforcement tools are often divided into "reactive detection methods" and "proactive detection methods". The former includes methods that rely on evidence and information that competition authorities receive from third parties, with leniency and whistle-blower programs amongst them. The second category would refer to initiatives of competition authorities when they undertake a proactive approach to detecting cartels without relying on external hints, including screening tools, market studies, and empirical economic analysis. Nonetheless, the emergence of new technological systems helps competition authorities to innovate and improve their available tools to fight competition law infringements as well as creating new opportunities that can help regulators to enforce competition law more efficiently[63].

What is more, a general interest in "computational antitrust" is rising amongst competition authorities, that is to say, competition law enforcement that relies on sophisticated ADM tools, with some competition authorities in Europe indicating even the creation of *ad hoc* digital units. For instance, the Italian Competition Authority has developed a pilot project aiming at collecting data from popular e-commerce platforms and monitoring their ranking algorithms with data analysis, web scraping, AI and machine learning techniques. The study was conducted on Amazon, and with the development of a supervised machine learning algorithm, "Random Forest" in an attempt to monitor e-commerce platforms that hold a dominant position in the market and investigate potential competition infringements, such as discrimination and collusion. This would be a perfect example of the development of proactive detection methods and is used for decisions on the initiation of an enforcement procedure[64].

Similarly, the Greek Competition Authority has established a Forensic Investigation Detection Unit composed of economists and data scientists and has put in place a platform in charge of collecting publicly available data on different products to observe trends in price changes over a time series (daily, weekly, etc.). An algorithmic screening tool is then employed to monitor the prices of a single product offered by different sellers to identify suspicious behaviour that may require further investigation.

The UK Competition and Markets Authority (CMA) has equally enhanced its approach through innovative measures, notably by establishing a specialized unit called Data, Technology, and Analysis (DaTA). Comprising

61   *Ibid.*

62   Smuha, N.A. (2021). "From a 'race to AI' to a 'race to AI regulation': regulatory competition for artificial intelligence", *Law, Innovation and Technology*, Vol. 13, Iss. 1.

63   Hofmann, H. and Lorenzoni, I. (2023). "Future Challenges for Automation in Competition Law Enforcement", *Stanford Computational Antitrust*, Vol. III, pp.38-41.

64   *Ibid.*

experts in data science, law, and economics, this unit aims to deepen comprehension of how corporate algorithms operate and how they leverage collected data. Its primary mandate is to oversee compliance with competition and consumer laws. Initially deployed in cases of consumer law violations, AI systems overseen by the DaTA unit are now also utilized in antitrust and merger cases. For instance, natural language processing techniques are employed to scrutinize internal company documents. These AI systems are integrated into both proactive and reactive enforcement strategies, strategically utilized at various stages of an enforcement process, primarily during investigations prompted by suspicions of wrongdoing.

In last instance, the Spanish Competition Authority has established an Economic Intelligence Unit since 2018, tasked with developing innovative computational tools for detecting various forms of anticompetitive practices, including algorithmic collusion. As per an OECD report, this unit employs advanced statistical, econometric, network analysis, and machine learning techniques, both supervised and unsupervised. These methodologies are primarily applied to identify bid rigging cartels in the public procurement domain, given its data-rich nature. The utilization of AI primarily revolves around uncovering and investigating potential breaches of competition law.

5.2. Detection

These last examples prove the intent by competition authorities to implement computational antitrust measures, introducing machine learning algorithms with pattern recognition and prediction-making features. Digital tools of the sort are mainly implemented to assess large data pools, and in particular, machine learning has the potential to detect suspicious patterns of behaviour on markets or co-relations between various data points.

However, in public enforcement said technological tools have different uses depending on the phase on the enforcement procedure, which are: an initiation phase, investigation, decision making and implementation.

One of the most common computational tools in competition law enforcement are "screenings". Screening refers to a process whereby industries where the existence of a cartel is likely (structural screens) are identified, or to examine whether firms' behaviour in a market are the result of a collusion (behavioural screens). Even if screenings do not amount to tools that provide direct evidence of collusion, they are useful to raise flags on unusual behaviours that could be a consequence of anticompetitive practices, although they require an intense number of resources. Such screen tools have proven useful in the detection of cartels for instance in the field of fuel retail markets[65] and in bid rigging structures in public procurement[66]. These tools recollect historical data of past competition cases and then calculate predictions in the same area on the likelihood of collusion.

At the same time, machine learning systems are supposed to, as the author Lianos[67] argues, "provide the possibility to find nontrivial collusive patterns that econometrics could not foresee and they may build non-trivial tests on these patterns[68]. In fact, the success of machine learning at intelligence tasks is largely due to its ability to discover complex structures that were not specified in advance. Nonetheless, some competition authorities concede that one of the main challenges as regards benefitting from existing technology is the availability and quality of market data rather than the hardware. Machine learning algorithms require data sets with large data on collusion and non-collusion scenarios, on price, cost and drivers of supply and demand, and a large part of this data are companies' private data, which become a barrier to fully operational machine learning algorithms. Such asymmetries between regulators and private companies could result in disruptive changes in competition law enforcement.

Secondly, during the investigation phase, competition authorities implement document management software to handle large volumes of data, employing digitalization to enhance efficiency. This includes sophisticated tools like

65   Silveira, D., Vasconcelos, S., Resende, M. and Cajueiro, D. O. (2022). "Won't Get Fooled Again: A Supervised Machine Learning Approach for Screening Gasoline Cartels", *105 Energy Econ.* 1. Available at: https://www.sciencedirect.com/science/article/pii/S0140988321005594 [14/04/2024].

66   Huber, M. and Imhof, D. (2019). "Machine Learning with Screens for Detecting Bid-Rigging Cartels", *International Journal of Industrial Organisation*, Vol 65, p. 277-301. Available at: https://doi.org/10.1016/j.ijindorg.2019.04.002 [14/04/2024].

67   Lianos, I. (2021). "Computational Competition Law and Economics: Issues, Prospects - An Inception Report", *Hellenic Competition Commission.*

68   Idem.

machine learning-based solutions with pattern recognition capabilities. For example, the European Commission issues Search Query Requests for Information (RFI) to companies, requiring specific documents based on keywords. However, privacy and legal professional privilege (LPP) must be ensured before sharing documents. Consequently, some law firms are developing in-house search tools with machine learning AI to recognize LPP-protected documents. Additionally, the Swedish Competition Authority is also exploring natural language processing for anonymizing texts and identifying protected documents.

Concerns arise regarding the right of parties to access their files, particularly when AI is involved, due to the complexity and opacity of machine learning. What is more, defining relevant markets in competition law investigations could equally benefit from computational tools. Econometric models, encouraged by the Commission, could be enhanced with screening tools and deep learning techniques to understand market dynamics. However, challenges include explainability of AI models and supervision of machine learning reliant markets. Regulators would need high data retention and supervisory AI technology, which currently lacks infrastructure.

As regards the decision-making phase, enforcing competition law can involve requesting behavioural changes and imposing fines on companies for infringement. Machine learning algorithms trained on past antitrust cases are being developed to assist regulators in this process by analyzing previous decisions to identify patterns and factors influencing outcomes, aiding in shaping future decisions. Machine learning's ability to process vast amounts of data quickly is a significant advantage. Additionally, computational tools could automate the monitoring phase, particularly for online companies, ensuring compliance with remedies such as restricting certain content on web pages.

5.3. Accountability

In real life competition enforcement, we come across an interplay between human action and automated decision-making algorithms, where the boundaries between both are not always clear. Such integration of ADM into decision-making procedures tends to be described as "quasi- or semi-automated decision-making" and concerns the quantity of information and the speed at which it can be processed (quantitative effects) but also the quality and depth by which information can be analyzed (qualitative effects). However, ADM are gradually being introduced in specific phases rather than to the whole decision-making process. However, the use of ADM technologies in one phase of decision-making could potentially limit the discretion of human decision-makers in subsequent phases. Moreover, in case of errors, officers relying on ADM may not be considered to have acted wrongly, while those challenging ADM decisions would face higher scrutiny in justifying their actions. This hierarchical dynamic could further complicate decision-making processes for individual case handlers.

The accountability of decision-making with ADM systems also poses challenges. The Court of Justice of the European Union emphasizes the right to a reasoned decision, which necessitates demonstrating compliance with essential procedural requirements. This includes providing adequate reasons for decisions, enabling individuals to understand the basis of decisions and defend their rights effectively. Failure to provide adequate reasons may breach the duty of care, leading to potential annulment of measures contested in court.

While we are aware of the data that the algorithm uses to reach a decision, the opaqueness of the reasons why the algorithm adopts a certain decision remains problematic. Consequently, several fundamental rights may be at risk, including the right to an effective remedy as stipulated by Article 47 Charter of Fundamental Rights of the European Union ("EU Charter").

Article 47 of the EU Charter guarantees the right to a fair trial, which includes access to a public hearing before an impartial tribunal within a reasonable time frame. In cases where governments employ Automated Decision-Making systems such right can be compromised, and it must be acknowledged that it's crucial for proceedings to be adversarial, allowing parties to review and respond to documents and arguments presented by the other side. The judiciary must ensure equality between the parties, granting them a fair opportunity to contest the evidence presented by the opposing party. Additionally, judges must provide reasoned decisions, enabling parties to understand the basis of the court's ruling and potentially appeal it. However, as previously developed, the opacity of algorithms used in ADM systems can hinder the fairness of trials, as judges may struggle to facilitate party participation and issue reasoned decisions.

The algorithms utilized in administrative ADM processes may be inexplicable, as demonstrated by the case of North Tyneside's where no explanation could be found by the English Metropolitan Borough of North Tyneside as to why certain applications for housing benefits were assigned a higher risk rating by the Risk Based Verification systems[69]. Furthermore, governments may refuse to disclose the algorithms for reasons such as preventing misuse or protecting intellectual property. Even if administrators are willing to share the algorithms, understanding their operation may be extremely difficult, as seen with Trelleborg's social benefits allocation algorithm. Consequently, judges and citizens are left uninformed about how administrative decisions are made, undermining the judiciary's ability to ensure fair trials[70].

5.4. Coordination between competition authorities

The intricate nature of AI applications in specific domains such as competition policy, financial markets, and healthcare suggests that a centralized regulatory approach may not be practical, as different aspects of machine learning require tailored oversight (Coglianese, 2023[92]). Consequently, there is a divergence in the legal frameworks being developed for AI, with some adopting stringent "hard law" measures (e.g., the EU AI Act), while others rely on softer guidelines, "soft law" measures (e.g., OECD AI guidelines) (Larsen and Yu, 2023[95]). As a result, effective governance demands that governments and policymakers collaborate and share their expertise with each other, in order to address the risks associated with AI.

Competition authorities stand to gain valuable insights by exchanging knowledge and collaborating with their counterparts globally. That is, given the expansive international reach of major digital corporations, regulatory bodies worldwide face parallel challenges in mitigating their negative impacts. Therefore, fostering cooperation among competition authorities is crucial, as emphasized by the Japan Fair Trade Commission (2021). This collaboration extends to sharing experiences and expertise through avenues like workshops and roundtables hosted by organizations such as the OECD and the International Competition Network. Additionally, jurisdictions are forging bilateral ties, as evidenced by the efforts outlined by the Competition & Markets Authority (2021).

Moreover, corporations sometimes extend commitments beyond individual jurisdictions where competition law violations occur, benefiting consumers globally. Notably, Google's global commitments in cases like the France *Autorité de la Concurrence* online advertising and the UK Competition and Markets Authority privacy sandbox underscore this trend.

Furthermore, competition authorities can draw lessons from regulators in other sectors facing analogous challenges. Several jurisdictions, including Australia, the Netherlands, and the UK, are adopting a coordinated approach to digital regulation across various sectoral regulators. This underscores the significance of regulators collaborating to enhance expertise, streamline operations, and reduce undue burdens on businesses. For instance, the UK Digital Regulation Cooperation Forum (DRCF) aims to enhance algorithmic transparency by bolstering sector regulators' capabilities for auditing algorithms and promoting transparency in algorithmic procurement. The UK government expects regulators to actively engage in implementing principles outlined in the proposed pro-innovation regulatory framework for AI (UK Department for Science, Innovation & Technology, 2023).

Other sector regulators often use regulatory sandboxes, with several examples across the OECD. "A regulatory sandbox refers to a limited form of regulatory waiver or flexibility for firms, enabling them to test new business models with reduced regulatory requirements. Sandboxes often include mechanisms intended to ensure overarching regulatory objectives, including consumer protection. Regulatory sandboxes are typically organised and administered on a case-by-case basis by the relevant regulatory authorities. Regulatory sandboxes have emerged in a range of sectors across the OECD and beyond, notably in finance but also in health, transport, legal services, aviation and energy" (OECD, 2020[96]).

---

69   Chiusi, F. (2020). "Automating Society Report". Available online at https://automatingsociety.algorithmwatch.org [14/04/2024].

70   De Heer, S. (2021). "Administrative Automated Decision-Making: What About the Right to an Effective Remedy?", *OxHRH Blog*. Available at: https://ohrh.law.ox.ac.uk/administrative-automated-decision-making-what-about-the-right-to-an-effective-remedy [14/04/2024].

Competition authorities stand to glean insights from the AI soft law initiatives. Presently, there lacks concrete "hard law" legal frameworks mandating AI conduct, with prevailing regulations primarily constituting soft law, encompassing agreements, principles, or declarations devoid of legal enforceability. The OECD AI Principles serve as a prime exemplar of such soft law, marking the inaugural set of global guidelines for AI, facilitated by the OECD's Working Party on Artificial Intelligence Governance (AIGO). These principles, formulated through collaboration with both civil society and industry stakeholders, set a precedent for international AI governance. Nonetheless, the impending EU AI Act is poised to pioneer the enactment of binding regulations governing AI on a significant scale globally. This legislation delineates the contours of an AI auditing framework, offering a blueprint for oversight and regulation in the AI realm. Given the rapid pace of AI advancements, governmental responses are expected to be swift and continuously evolving across jurisdictions.

In summary, with the advancing AI landscape, it is crucial for competition authorities, industry participants, and other involved parties to collaborate closely. Through active engagement and sharing of valuable perspectives, companies, academic institutions, and market stakeholders can influence antitrust policies that promote innovation, fairness, and consumer well-being in the age of AI. Armed with this input, authorities can make informed decisions on how to effectively address the dynamic and promising AI market.

Moreover, the new AI Office's mandate (a centralized EU agency within the European Commission) which began its operation on February 21, 2024, will be to: (a) ensure the uniform implementation and enforcement of the AI Act, particularly in relation to general-purpose AI ("GPAI") models; (b) support and monitor the development of AI markets and policies across the EU; and (c) develop and coordinate collaboration and cooperation initiatives within and outside the EU.

6. Conclusions

The digital marketplace is undergoing swift changes, witnessing a surge in the adoption of pricing algorithms. Although these algorithms offer numerous advantages, there exists a tangible danger that they may introduce fresh risks and complexities for regulators aiming to curb anti-competitive practices.

1. To date, there has unfortunately been comparatively little research into this area, and hence more is needed in order to detect patterns attributed to collusive outcomes as well as regular unlawful algorithmic behaviour. Going forward, further knowledge is needed for policymaking in this area. First of all, more empirical and economic research on the actual implementations of algorithmic pricing is required, as well as a deeper cooperation between competition authorities, entailing the removal of legal barriers to sharing technology and data. Moreover, the advanced nature of algorithms, particularly pricing algorithms, makes them appealing tools for businesses. They drastically improve the efficiency of price-setting compared to traditional methods, which were slower and relied on outdated data. With pricing algorithms, decisions that once took days or weeks can now be made in seconds with real-time data, offering considerable benefits for profit-maximizing enterprises. This efficiency is particularly attractive in sectors like e-commerce, where pricing algorithms are increasingly common.

2. However, the use of pricing algorithms also raises concerns. While they offer undeniable benefits, they can also facilitate explicit collusion, making agreements between businesses more efficient, and exacerbate the threat of tacit collusion. Tacit collusion involves a tacit meeting of minds, where existing competition law may apply. Nonetheless, the trends in the EU courts have been to view tacit collusion as not illegal per se unless it can be proven that an explicit agreement, decisions of undertakings or concerted practices that may lead to anti-competitive conduct occurred during such tacit collusion. The issue of appropriate remedies and measures to prohibit and tackle algorithmic collusion is addressed in the present work, which includes the expansion of the concept of agreement or concerted practices. The sophistication of pricing algorithms enables them to autonomously monitor and set prices based on market conditions, often resulting in prices that favor businesses over consumers. This raises questions about whether these optimal prices truly benefit consumers or merely serve the interests of profit-driven enterprises.

3. With all, the question is raised regarding whether existing competition law is sufficient to address the new scenarios of algorithmic collusion and their associated challenges. The first one is the Messenger Scenario, whereby algorithms act as facilitators of pre-existing human agreements, such as cartels. Traditional competition regulations can address these scenarios by focusing on the human intent to collude rather than the mechanics of how collusion is carried out. Secondly, we encounter the Hub-and-Spoke Scenario: In this setup, competing entities utilize an intermediary to orchestrate collusion, creating a façade of indirect collusion. Pricing algorithms play a crucial role in these cases, potentially leading to automatic price-fixing without explicit collusion among competitors.

Next, we come across the Predictable Agent Scenario, which, together with the final "Digital Eye" one, are the most challenging and innovative ones. They represent how tacit collusion can be amplified to a new level of stability and scope by key technological advancements. In a Predictable Agent Scenario, each undertaking develops its pricing algorithm with the aim to maximize profits. These algorithms often operate similarly, avoiding price wars and maintaining stable prices above competitive levels. The challenge lies in proving intent to collude when operators knowingly adopt algorithms that could lead to anti-competitive outcomes. Lastly, the Digital Eye Scenario utilizes AI as the foundation for pricing algorithms, enabling them to refine strategies autonomously. The opacity of decision-making in these algorithms poses significant challenges for competition authorities, as it complicates efforts to discern anti-competitive behavior.

These scenarios highlight the complexities of algorithmic collusion, ranging from facilitating pre-existing agreements to autonomously maximizing profits through self-learning algorithms. The challenges include detecting collusion in opaque decision-making processes, proving intent to collude, and balancing the interests of businesses and consumers in regulatory interventions. Each scenario requires nuanced approaches tailored to the specific challenges posed by algorithmic collusion in modern markets.

4. Additionally, we observe a growing adoption of artificial intelligence by competition authorities worldwide to bolster their enforcement capacities in scrutinizing possible breaches of competition law. This transition towards what is known as "computational antitrust" entails deploying advanced algorithms, screenings, document management software, data analysis, machine learning methods, and other AI-driven techniques to actively pinpoint anticompetitive actions like collusion and discrimination, and to enhance and assist in different phases of the enforcement process, such as initiation, investigation, decision-making, and implementation. Screenings, for instance, help identify industries or behaviors that may indicate collusion, while machine learning algorithms analyze large data pools to detect suspicious patterns of behavior or correlations between data points. In particular, several competition authorities across Europe, including Italy, Greece, and Spain, have established specialized units or initiatives aimed at developing and implementing digital tools for detecting anticompetitive practices, particularly algorithmic collusion.

5. However, challenges persist, particularly concerning data availability and quality, privacy concerns, and the complexity of AI models. Additionally, ensuring the explainability and supervision of AI models, as well as addressing the right of parties to access their files, are important considerations. Despite these challenges, the adoption of computational tools shows promise in enhancing the efficiency and effectiveness of competition law enforcement.

Privacy concerns in AI collusion and competition law stem from the potential exploitation of personal data and the risk of anti-competitive practices. AI systems utilized in these contexts often rely on extensive data sets, raising the specter of data misuse or unauthorized access. Transparency issues further compound these worries, as opaque algorithms make it challenging to understand how decisions are made and the extent to which personal data is utilized. Additionally, cross-platform tracking capabilities of AI systems exacerbate privacy risks by compiling detailed user profiles, potentially leading to invasive targeted advertising or manipulation of consumer choices. Moreover, the inherent biases in AI algorithms can perpetuate discrimination, posing further privacy challenges for marginalized groups.

To address these concerns, a multifaceted approach is necessary, encompassing stringent data protection regulations, enhanced algorithmic transparency measures, and ethical considerations embedded within AI design and deployment. Adherence to existing data protection laws such as GDPR or CCPA is crucial to safeguard individuals' privacy rights and ensure accountability for AI systems involved in collusion or competition law. Furthermore, promoting algorithmic transparency enables stakeholders to scrutinize AI decision-making processes, fostering trust and accountability. Ethical guidelines should guide the development and implementation of AI technologies, mitigating potential privacy risks and promoting responsible use in collusion and competition law contexts.

6. In essence, this study highlights the crucial need for a robust regulatory framework to thwart attempts to bypass existing regulations and manipulate legal loopholes for forming algorithmic cartels, as well as offer solutions to tackle such algorithmic collusion, even if they are not exhaustive. Each jurisdiction may adopt different approaches based on its legal framework and political will. Guidelines on AI, for example, could indirectly mitigate the harmful effects of algorithmic collusion, but complete eradication may require more radical measures. Ultimately, the approach taken will depend on each jurisdiction's unique circumstances and objectives in addressing the challenge of algorithmic collusion. It also stresses the significance of consistently reviewing and amending laws to keep pace with contemporary realities and advancements in AI. To address these imperatives, a more expansive legal structure could be crafted, enabling swifter detection of algorithmic collusion and more effective utilization of these technologies in identifying anti-competitive behaviour.

Bibliography

EUROPEAN COMMISSION (2024). "Commission launches calls for contributions on competition in virtual worlds and generative AI". European Commission Press Corner. Available at : https://ec.europa.eu/commission/presscorner/detail/en/IP_24_85 [14/04/2024].

MAGBAGBEOLA, T. (2022). "Algorithmic Collusion as Agreement and/or Concerted Practice under EU Competition Law of Article 101(1) Treaty of the Functioning of the European Union". *University of Oslo.*

ABDEL GHAFFAR, A. "Concerted practices", *Global Dictionary of Competition Law, Concurrences,* Art. N° 12332. Available at: https://www.concurrences.com/en/dictionary/Concerted-Practice [14/04/2024].

ALEKSANDRA LAMONTANARO, A. (2020). "Bounty Hunters For Algorithmic Cartels: An Old Solution for a New Problem", 30 *Fordham Intell. Prop. Media & Entertainment Law Journal,* 1259. Available at: https://ir.lawnet.fordham.edu/iplj/vol30/iss4/6 [14/04/2024].

ANTONIO GOMES, A. "CIP Talks... Interview with Antonio Gomes of the OECD".

EZRACHI, A. & STUCKE, M. E. (2016). 'Virtual Competition: The Promise and Perils of the Algorithm-Driven Economy', *Harvard University Press*, p. 21.

ASENSIO-SOTO, J. C., and NAVARRO-ASTOR, E. (2022). "Proptech: A qualitative analysis of online real estate brokerage agencies in Spain. Intangible Capital", *Intangible Capital,* Vol 18, N° 3, pp. 489-505. https://doi.org/10.3926/ic.2090

BOUCHER, P. (2020). "Artificial intelligence: How does it work, why does it matter, and what can we do about it?". *European Parliamentary Research Service,* Available at https://www.europarl.europa.eu/thinktank/en/document/EPRS_STU(2020)641547 [14/04/2024]

CALVANO, E., CALZOLARI, G., DENICOLÒ, V. and PASTORELLO, S. (2019). "Algorithmic Pricing What Implications for Competition Policy?", *Review of Industrial Organisation.* Available at: https://doi.org/10.1007/s11151-019-09689-3 [14/04/2024].

CHIUSI, F. (2020). "Automating Society Report". Available online at: https://automatingsociety.algorithmwatch.org [14/04/2024].

CID MORALES, M. T. (2017). "La colusión y los acuerdos horizontales: Programa de Clemencia", *Facultade de Ciencias Empresariais e Turismo de Ourense,* p. 8 et *sqq./seq.*

DE HEER, S. (2021). "Administrative Automated Decision-Making: What About the Right to an Effective Remedy?", *OxHRH Blog.* Available at: https://ohrh.law.ox.ac.uk/administrative-automated-decision-making-what-about-the-right-to-an-effective-remedy [14/04/2024].

DOBRIN, S. (2019). "Algorithms and Collusion: Competition Law Challenges of Pricing Algorithms", *Faculty of Law of Lund University.*

EUROPEAN COMMISSION (2018). "Commission fines four consumer electronics manufacturers for fixing online resale prices", *European Commission Press Corner.* Available at: https://ec.europa.eu/commission/presscorner/detail/en/IP_18_4601 [14/04/2024].

EZRACHI, A. and STUCKE, M. E. (2019). "The Promise and Perils of the Algorithm-Driven Economy", *Virtual Competition,* (n 47), ch 7.

FOUNTOUKAKOS, K. "Cartel". *Global Dictionary of Competition Law, Concurrences,* Art. N° 12240. Available at: https://www.concurrences.com/en/dictionary/cartel

GATA, J. E. (2021). "Collusion between Algorithms: A Literature Review and Limits to Enforcement". *European Review of Business Economics I(1),* pp. 73-94; DOI: https://doi.org/10.26619/ERBE2021.01.4

GOODMAN, J. M., THEODOSIOU, L. and CECCIO, J. (2023). "Antitrust Agencies Identify Generative Ai Concerns". *Competition Policy International, Regulating Generative Artificial Intelligence,* Volume 2, pp. 3-6.

HARRINGTON, J. E. and YE, L. (2019). "Collusion through Coordination of Announcements", *The Journal of Industrial Economics*, Volume 67, Issue 2, pp. 209-241.

HAWKES, C. (2021). "A Market Investigation Tool to Tackle Algorithmic Tacit Collusion: An Approach for the (Near) Future", *College of Europe.*

HOFMANN, H. and LORENZONI, I. (2023). "Future Challenges for Automation in Competition Law Enforcement", *Stanford Computational Antitrust*, Vol. III, pp. 38-41.

HUA, S. & BELFIELD, H. (2021). "Ai & Antitrust: Reconciling Tensions Between Competition Law And Cooperative Ai Development", *Yale Journal of Law & Technology, 23,* pp. 415 et sqq./seq.

HUBER, M. & IMHOF, D. (2019). "Machine Learning with Screens for Detecting Bid-Rigging Cartels", *International Journal of Industrial Organisation*, Vol. 65, pp. 277-301. Available at: https://doi.org/10.1016/j.ijindorg.2019.04.002 [14/04/2024].

HUNT, M., SCHERF, R. and BURAK DARBAZ, S. (2022). "Self-Preferencing in Digital Markets", *Global Competition Review.* Available at: https://globalcompetitionreview.com/guide/digital-markets-guide/second-edition/article/self-preferencing-in-digital-markets

IVALDI, M., JULLIEN, B., REY, P., SEABRIGHT, P., and TIROLE, J. (2003). "The economics of Tacit Collusion horizontal mergers: Unilateral and coordinated effects". *DG Competition, European Commission.*

LIANOS, I. (2021). "Computational Competition Law and Economics: Issues, Prospects-An Inception Report", *Hellenic Competition Commission.*

MAURIE, K. (2020). "Pricing Algorithms: Should Competition Authorities be Worried?". *European Law Blog.* Available at: https://europeanlawblog.eu/2020/12/21/pricing-algorithms-should-competition-authorities-be-worried/

ODUDU O. (2006). "The Boundaries of EC Competition Law: The Scope of Article 81", *Oxford Academic Books.*

OECD (2021). "OECD Business and Finance Outlook 2021: AI Business and Finance", *OECD iLibrary*, Available at: https://www.oecd-ilibrary.org/sites/3acbe1cd-en/index.html?itemId=/content/component/3acbe1cd-en [08/04/2024].

PAGE, W. H. (2007). "Communication and Concerted Action" 38 Loy. U. Chi. L.J. 405. Available at http://scholarship.law.ufl.edu/facultypub/97

PETIT, N. (2017). "Antitrust and Artificial Intelligence: A Research Agenda, Journal of European Competition Law & Practice". *Journal of European Competition Law & Practice*, Volume 8, Issue 6, p. 361–362. Available at: https://doi.org/10.1093/jeclap/lpx033

ROBERT, L. H. and MARVEL, H. (2000). "The Three Types of Collusion: Fixing Prices, Rivals, and Rules", *Wis. L. Rev. 941, University of Baltimore School of Law.*

SILVEIRA, D., VASCONCELOS, S., RESENDE, M. & CAJUEIRO, D. O. (2022). "Won't Get Fooled Again: A Supervised Machine Learning Approach for Screening Gasoline Cartels", *105 Energy Econ.* 1. Available at: https://www.sciencedirect.com/science/article/pii/S0140988321005594 [14/04/2024].

SLOVER, G. (2023). "Is Artificial Intelligence a New Gateway to Anticompetitive Collusion?". *Center for Democracy & Technology.* Available at: https://cdt.org/insights/is-artificial-intelligence-a-new-gateway-to-anticompetitive-collusion/ [14/04/2024]

SMUHA, N. A. (2021). "From a 'race to AI' to a 'race to AI regulation': regulatory competition for artificial intelligence", *Law, Innovation and Technology*, Vol. 13, Iss. 1.

Case Law

European Court of Justice of the European Union

– [2018] OJ C 335/05. See also Denon & Marantz (Case AT.40469) Commission Decision C(2018) 4774 final [2018].

– 338/08. See also ASUS (Case AT.40465) Commission Decision C(2018) 4773 final [2018].

– Asus (vertical restraints) (Case AT.40465) Summary of Commission Decision C/2018/4773 [2018] OJ C.

– C-199/92 P - Hüls v Commission.

– C-89/85 Ahlström Osakeyhtiö, ECLI:EU:C:1993:120 ("Wood Pulp"), para. 71.

– Case AT.39740 Google Search (Shopping), 27 June 2017, available at: https://ec.europa.eu/competition/antitrust/cases/dec_docs/39740/39740_14996_3.pdf

– Case C-286/13P Dole Food Co Inc v Commission (2015) EU:C: 2015:184; Case T-588/08 P, Dole Food and Dole Germany v Commission (2013) EU: T:2013:130.

– Case C-74/14 "Eturas" UAB and Others v Lietuvos Respublikos konkurencijos taryba (Eturas) EU:C:2016:42. Available at : https://curia.europa.eu/juris/liste.jsf?&num=C-74/14 [14/04/2024].

– Case C-74/14 "Eturas" UAB and Others v Lietuvos Respublikos konkurencijos taryba (Eturas) EU:C:2016:42.

– Case C-8/08 T-Mobile Netherlands and Others (2009) EU:C: 2009:343.

– Case C-89/85, A. Ahlström Osakeyhtiö and others v Commission (Woodpulp II).

– Case T- 41/96, Bayer AG v. Commission 69.

– Case T-35/92, John Deere Ltd v Commission EU:T:1994:259; Case C-7/95 P, John Deere Ltd v Commission EU:C:1998:256.

– Cases T- 25/95, Cimenteries CBR and Others v Commission ECLI:EU:T:2000:77 (March 15, 2020).

– Denon & Marantz (vertical restraints) (Case AT.40469) Summary of Commission Decision C/2018/4774.

– Dyestuffs, Imperial Chemical Industries Ltd v Commission of the European Communities, Final judgment, 48/69, (1972) ECR 619, ILEC 036 (CJEU 1972), 14th July 1972, Court of Justice of the European Union [CJEU]; European Court of Justice [ECJ].

– EU Court of Justice, AC-Treuhand, Case C-194/14 P, 22 October 2015.

– Joined Cases 40–48, 50, 54–56, 111, 113 & 114/73 Suiker Unie" UA and others v Commission.

– Philips (vertical restraints) (Case AT.40181) Summary of Commission Decision C/2018/4797 [2018] OJ C 340/07. See also Philips (Case AT.40181) Commission Decision C(2018) 4797 final [2018].

– Pioneer (vertical restraints) (Case AT.40182) Summary of Commission Decision C/2018/4790 [2018] OJ C 338/11. See also Pioneer (Case AT.40182) Commission Decision C(2018) 4790 final [2018].

Legislation and other official documents

– (2021). "Commission Notice on the definition of relevant market for the purposes of Community competition law of 9 December 1997", *European Commission*.

– European Commission. "Guidelines on the applicability of Article 101 of the Treaty on the Functioning of the European Union to horizontal co-operation agreements", para 61.

– See eg the EC Merger Regulation, para 25; Commission, 'Guidelines on the assessment of horizontal mergers under the Council Regulation on the control of concentrations between undertakings' (Horizontal Merger Guidelines) (2004/C 31/03), para 22.

Números Publicados
Serie Unión Europea y Relaciones Internacionales

Nº 1/2000 «La política monetaria única de la Unión Europea»
Rafael Pampillón Olmedo

Nº 2/2000 «Nacionalismo e integración»
Leonardo Caruana de las Cagigas y Eduardo González Calleja

Nº 1/2001 «Standard and Harmonize: Tax Arbitrage»
Nohemi Boal Velasco y Mariano González Sánchez

Nº 2/2001 «Alemania y la ampliación al este: convergencias y divergencias»
José María Beneyto Pérez

Nº 3/2001 «Towards a common European diplomacy? Analysis of the European Parliament resolution
on establishing a common diplomacy (A5-0210/2000)»
Belén Becerril Atienza y Gerardo Galeote Quecedo

Nº 4/2001 «La Política de Inmigración en la Unión Europea»
Patricia Argerey Vilar

Nº 1/2002 «ALCA: Adiós al modelo de integración europea?»
Mario Jaramillo Contreras

Nº 2/2002 «La crisis de Oriente Medio: Palestina»
Leonardo Caruana de las Cagigas

Nº 3/2002 «El establecimiento de una delimitación más precisa de las competencias entre la Unión Europea
y los Estados miembros»
José María Beneyto y Claus Giering

Nº 4/2002 «La sociedad anónima europea»
Manuel García Riestra

Nº 5/2002 «Jerarquía y tipología normativa, procesos legislativos y separación de poderes en la Unión Europea:
hacia un modelo más claro y transparente»
Alberto Gil Ibáñez

Nº 6/2002 «Análisis de situación y opciones respecto a la posición de las Regiones en el ámbito de la UE.
Especial atención al Comité de las Regiones»
Alberto Gil Ibáñez

Nº 7/2002 «Die Festlegung einer genaueren Abgrenzung der Kompetenzen zwischen der Europäischen Union
und den Mitgliedstaaten»
José María Beneyto y Claus Giering

Nº 1/2003 «Un español en Europa. Una aproximación a Juan Luis Vives»
José Peña González

Nº 2/2003 «El mercado del arte y los obstáculos fiscales ¿Una asignatura pendiente en la Unión Europea?»
Pablo Siegrist Ridruejo

Nº 1/2004 «Evolución en el ámbito del pensamiento de las relaciones España-Europa»
José Peña González

Nº 2/2004 «La sociedad europea: un régimen fragmentario con intención armonizadora»
Alfonso Martínez Echevarría y García de Dueñas

Nº 3/2004 «Tres operaciones PESD: Bosnia y Herzegovina, Macedonia y República Democrática de Congo»
Berta Carrión Ramírez

Serie Política de la Competencia y Regulación

Nº 1/2001   «El control de concentraciones en España: un nuevo marco legislativo para las empresas»
José María Beneyto

Nº 2/2001   «Análisis de los efectos económicos y sobre la competencia de la concentración Endesa-Iberdrola»
Luis Atienza, Javier de Quinto y Richard Watt

Nº 3/2001   «Empresas en Participación concentrativas y artículo 81 del Tratado CE: Dos años de aplicación
del artículo 2(4) del Reglamento CE de control de las operaciones de concentración»
Jerónimo Maíllo González-Orús

Nº 1/2002   «Cinco años de aplicación de la Comunicación de 1996 relativa a la no imposición de multas
o a la reducción de su importe en los asuntos relacionados con los acuerdos entre empresas»
Miguel Ángel Peña Castellot

Nº 1/2002   «Leniency: la política de exoneración del pago de multas en derecho de la competencia»
Santiago Illundaín Fontoya

Nº 3/2002   «Dominancia vs. disminución sustancial de la competencia ¿cuál es el criterio más apropiado?:
aspectos jurídicos»
Mercedes García Pérez

Nº 4/2002   «Test de dominancia vs. test de reducción de la competencia: aspectos económicos»
Juan Briones Alonso

Nº 5/2002   «Telecomunicaciones en España: situación actual y perspectivas»
Bernardo Pérez de León Ponce

Nº 6/2002   «El nuevo marco regulatorio europeo de las telecomunicaciones»
Jerónimo González González y Beatriz Sanz Fernández-Vega

Nº 1/2003   «Some Simple Graphical Interpretations of the Herfindahl-Hirshman Index and their Implications»
Richard Watt y Javier De Quinto

Nº 2/2003   «La Acción de Oro o las privatizaciones en un Mercado Único»
Pablo Siegrist Ridruejo, Jesús Lavalle Merchán y Emilia Gargallo González

Nº 3/2003   «El control comunitario de concentraciones de empresas y la invocación de intereses nacionales.
Crítica del artículo 21.3 del Reglamento 4064/89»
Pablo Berenguer O'Shea y Vanessa Pérez Lamas

Nº 1/2004   «Los puntos de conexión en la Ley 1/2002 de 21 de febrero de coordinación de las competencias
del Estado y las Comunidades Autónomas en materia de defensa de la competencia»
Lucana Estévez Mendoza

Nº 2/2004   «Los impuestos autonómicos sobre los grandes establecimientos comerciales
como ayuda de Estado ilícita ex art. 87 TCE»
Francisco Marcos

Nº 1/2005   «Servicios de Interés General y Artículo 86 del Tratado CE: Una Visión Evolutiva»
Jerónimo Maillo González-Orús

Nº 2/2005   «La evaluación de los registros de morosos por el Tribunal de Defensa de la Competencia»
Alfonso Rincón García Loygorri